Managing People Acro.

This book is dedicated to Aelwyn and Bridget Rees, and Harold and Esther Garrison

Managing People Across Europe

Edited by
Terry Garrison
and
David Rees

Butterworth-Heinemann Ltd
Linacre House, Jordan Hill, Oxford OX2 8DP

A member of the Reed Elsevier plc group

OXFORD LONDON BOSTON
MUNICH NEW DELHI SINGAPORE SYDNEY
TOKYO TORONTO WELLINGTON

First published 1994

© Butterworth-Heinemann Ltd 1994

British Library Cataloguing in Publication Data
Managing People Across Europe
  I. Garrison, Terry   II. Rees, David
  658.3

ISBN 0 7506 1570 2

Typeset by Graphicraft Typesetters (HK) Ltd
Printed in Great Britain by Clays, St Ives plc

Contents

Contributors

Flemming Agersnap is Professor of Organizational Studies at the Copenhagen Business School where he specializes in industrial democracy in Europe and business strategy. He is currently involved in a joint project with Cranfield School of Management focusing on management process for strategy development.

Anton Artemyev is a management consultant working with the French group Siar-Bossard. He was, until 1992, a professor at the International Management Institute in St Petersburg.

Karl Blum is a professor at the Osnabrück Fachhochschule where he specializes in European economics. He is the author of two books in this field and has carried out considerable research work in China, where he is a visiting professor at the Union University, Hefei.

Angel Diaz is Chief Executive Officer of the Advanced Management Services Group at the Instituto de Estudios Superiores de la Empresa, University of Navarra, Spain. He also acts as an advisor to Spanish small and medium-sized enterprises in organizational and human resource management.

Terry Garrison lectures at Henley Management College where he is lead tutor in international business management and public services strategy on Henley's worldwide Distance Learning MBA. He is the author of *European Business Strategy* (Elm, 1994, 4th edition).

Paddy Miller is Professor of Management at the International Graduate School of Management, University of Navarra, Spain, where he specializes in the management of change. A prolific writer, he has recently produced a unique change and leadership course for MBA programmes in Germany, USA, France and Spain.

Kurt H. Parkum is Director of Undergraduate Studies at Pennsylvania State University, formerly directing the MBA programme there. Previously a

Fulbright professor at Copenhagen School of Business, he has published in the areas of voluntarism and health care administration.

David Rees is Director of the Centre for International Communication and Visiting Teaching Fellow at Henley Management College where he tutors on MBA Managing People programmes. He is also a consultant to several major international companies in management development and strategic change.

Velimir Srica is a visiting professor of Management Information Systems and Economic Cybernetics at People's University, Beijing and Florida State University. He has also held professorial appointments at the University of Zagreb, University of Rijeka and Zagreb Business School. He is the author or co-author of twenty-three books and over 200 articles in scientific and business journals.

Philippe Trouvé is a professor at the Ecole Superieure de Commerce in Clermont Ferrand where he directs the Master's Programme in European Human Resources Management. He specializes in the field of qualifications research.

Shaun Tyson is Head of the Human Resource Management Department at Cranfield University and has published widely in the field of human resources management. He is a member of the British Academy of Management.

Paul Verveen is currently working as an international consultant in the Caribbean and Middle-America, having been former Director of Henley Nederland Management College in Zeist. He specializes in human resource development and international management.

Preface

More and more British and continental European companies are now finding themselves under increasing pressure to compete more effectively. However, as they expand their area of European operations, they are becoming increasingly drawn into situations in which their existing high competence levels are suspect. Some now recognize a need to deal with a major gap in their knowledge: managing across cultures. Strong evidence exists that even the most senior managers in some leading companies do not know and understand enough of how their staff are managed – and can be managed – in different European countries where their companies operate. An explanation of the reasons for such differences in managerial approaches is the key focus of this book.

The need for increased insights is not restricted to existing managers. A new generation of European executives is coming into existence who will be expected to understand – and naturally respond to – intercultural differences, since their work will involve them managing integrated European operations. For them cultural awareness and sensitivity will be an everyday reality and not the result of remedial learning. This book creates a platform of knowledge for both types of manager.

Managing People Across Europe is therefore intended to be a significant contribution to the body of literature in two areas. The first is that of the learning organization – the company that deliberately modifies its management approaches and culture to enable it to cope better with developments taking place in its operating environment, on the basis of feedback from that very environment. The second area is that of the transnational corporation and the way in which it tackles the task of intercultural management.

The requirements of European business in the twenty-first century are for enhanced individual and corporate sensitivity in both these areas. A particular finding expressed in many of the country chapters of this book is the need for in-depth understanding of what could be called the politico-economic 'bedrock determinants of business culture' as well as the 'superstructural elements' of how managers behave in their own individualistic country systems.

It is certainly the direct experience of the editors of this book that many European managers have a total absence of any 'real feeling for' the essence of different managerial approaches used in other countries and, perhaps more significantly, understand very little of the ideological values and macro-systems which contextualize the business culture of a given country.

This is a serious problem. For business success in an increasingly tense, trade bloc-competitive world it is now vital for senior mangers, immersed through education and experience in the politico-economic system of one country, to have an empathy with that of others.

Japan, and its corporate approach to business management, is an excellent example. European countries fail to appreciate that Japanese success is not simply a matter of excellent management of the superstructure of business (through such artefacts as total quality management, *ringi* and so on) but also of a powerful substructure of tight and mutually profitable corporate relationships among government, the financial services community and industry. Increasing reliance on Japanese-style management practices plus an increased activation of the *laissez-faire* economic model are not necessarily going to be the answer to Britain's trade ills. Nor, for that matter, is German or French unwillingness to adjust their own particular business approach of heavy protection of workers and company ownership necessarily appropriate against a background of rising world competitiveness, involving such phenomena as outsourcing and downsizing.

The current changes taking place in the European and global trade scenario make this book even more relevant. The impact of success or failure in the Uruguay Round of GATT talks is uppermost in the minds of senior executives in European companies like Siemens, Ericsson, Alsthom or the Russian Kamaz. 'What to do in Europe itself, given the way the talks could work out' is the key issue which is becoming a significant change driver. This is occurring in two ways. The first relates to the strategic nature of a company's workforce while the second affects mergers, takeovers and alliances of companies who might have antipathetic, even alien, cultures.

For these reasons, a text which indicates the extent of differentials in European business cultures and explains their genesis will, we hope, be found very welcome by managers who are now faced with the urgent task of understanding the ways of foreign business. This compendium of contributions from the UK, France, Germany, Spain, Scandinavia, Central Europe, Russia and the Netherlands also bears testimony to such differences in business orientation and practice through the particular styles of writing and ordering of topics by the writers selected. They each reflect their own national interests.

'Autres pays, autres moeurs' says the French proverb. That is what this book has been designed to explore.

Terry Garrison
David Rees

Acknowledgements

The editors would like to offer their generous thanks to employees at the Centre for International Communication, Christchurch, who contributed to the preparation of the final manuscripts for this book. The following people are especially thanked for their help: Mandy Beenham, Claude Gameiro, Philippa Hale, Ellie Piot, Elaine Rees and Joe Wright.

Gratitude is also extended to Ann Garrison for her valued expertise in proofreading the drafts.

1 Managing people across Europe: an introductory framework

Terry Garrison

Cases in point

At first sight, the labour problems suffered in early 1993 by the American Hoover Company at its vacuum cleaner factory in Dijon, France, are an unlikely place to begin to construct an introductory framework for this book. It is the case, however, that they graphically illustrate one of the salient features of the tasks faced by those managing people across Europe – the existence within the European Union of national business cultures, and associated work practices, which are hugely dissimilar. This is our key focus and Hoover's predicament and strategy are highly instructive.

The case concerns a decision by Hoover to sack 700 production staff at its French factory and, for reasons of maintaining competitiveness, transfer production of its products to its factory in Scotland. Here, in Cambuslang, Hoover workers had already agreed to more competitive pay rates and working conditions and, as a result, 400 new jobs were to be created. So far as the company and its Scottish workforce were concerned, the decision was one based on the economics of comparative production costs. Overall labour costs, inclusive of 'social charges' (e.g. social security payments by the company), were said by the company to be 40 per cent cheaper in Scotland than in France.[1] Just how different average labour costs were in 1991 in leading industrial countries can be seen by reviewing the data in Table 1.1.

Hoover's approach was paralleled by Grundig who, also in 1993, decided to move the production of television sets from the factory in Creutzwald (Moselle) to Austria, much to the disgust of the French union Force Ouvrière de la Metallurgie and for much the same cost-reduction reasons. Table 1.1 provides a useful comparison of manufacturing costs.

The Hoover move was not widely seen as particularly remarkable in Britain. It was, indeed, welcomed by the government as a sign of economic progress. In contrast, it provoked considerable and widespread outrage in France. Socialist President Mitterand himself referred to it as 'job-stealing

Table 1.1 Comparative manufacturing costs[2]

US ($ per hour), average	Pay for time worked	Holiday pay and bonuses	Non-wage labour costs (A)	Total labour costs (B)	(A) as a % of (B)
EC	9.92	2.95	4.08	16.95	24.1
Germany	12.67	4.63	4.87	22.17	22.0
Italy	8.66	3.04	5.48	17.18	31.9
France	8.34	2.56	4.36	15.26	28.6
UK	9.88	1.60	1.94	13.42	14.5
Spain	9.03		3.62	12.65	28.6
Non-EU countries					
US	11.33	1.00	3.12	15.45	20.2
Japan	8.38	4.14	1.89	14.41	13.1
Asian NIES[a]	3.82		0.38	4.21	9.0

[a] Excludes training recruitment costs and subsidised canteens.
Hong Kong, South Korea, Singapore.
Source: CBI staff estimates based on US Bureau of Labor Statistics, June 1992 and other reports.

banditry' while the right-wing *France Soir* commented that, from this experience, France had drawn the lesson that 'Europe [as an entity] does not exist: the law of each one for himself prevails as soon as important interests are at stake'.[1]

Many French commentators advanced the view that the Social Chapter of the European Union's Maastricht treaty had been designed specifically and precisely to prevent such 'social dumping'. This was, of course, an element of the accord from which Britain had taken great pains to opt out. To underline its criticism of Hoover's managerial approach and the British government's negative stance on workers' rights the French Communist newspaper *L'Humanité* sought to whip up sentiment by labelling the Dijon workers as 'the children of Maastricht'.[1]

This was not the only example of what the French were coming to refer to as 'the two-culture shock'.[3] The focus of attention in 1993 on the long-running French 'social conflict' at paper makers Kimberly–Clark–Sopalin[4] was not, however, the transfer of jobs out of France so much as the perceived high-handed Anglo-Saxon way in which the management had issued a major restructuring plan without adequate consideration of the workers' views. This was a topic of great interest in France at the time because of the imminence of the French general elections – in which the Socialists lost heavily – and the impact of the recession in France which was itself provoking mass redundancies.

At tyre manufacturers Michelin, for example, almost 10 per cent of jobs were lost.[5] The critical issue in this case was, however, the extent to which the firm was working within a highly structured 'social plan', involving considerable 'social dialogue' to deal with the problem based on negotiation with the unions (here the CFDT, FO and CGT) and the government, and not addressing matters arbitrarily.

French critics of the British approach could find even more ammunition to support their arguments in the case of Timex, again in Scotland. Here, the company simply replaced high-cost, unionized labour with a lower-cost, non-unionized workforce in order to try desperately to remain competitive. The result was heavy, long-lasting and acrimonious picketing of the firm's premises and mass intimidation of the new workers which ultimately ended in the closure of the plant.

This is not to suggest, of course, that other European workforces were reacting differently from the French to similar problems at that time. In Germany, in early 1993, the members of the IG Metall Union threatened prolonged strike action if the employers failed to honour their previous agreement to raise wages and salaries in East Germany to the level of those in the West within a specified time period. This was despite the elaborate, time-honoured system of detailed social-economic negotiations among the stakeholders in German industry and commerce – government, employers and unions.

The point is not one of the precise results in these and other cases involving different aspects of working practices but how they fail to reflect a common managerial approach to these issues. As we shall see, not only do these practices vary considerably but they are also often the product of business cultures which have developed over history in such radically different ways that they seem almost to defy the homogenization of working life which is central to mainland Europe's aspirations for the future political and economic development of the European Union.

EU differences

One of these critical divergences between countries' approaches to the management of work was amply illustrated at the meeting of a Council of Ministers in Luxembourg on 1 June 1993. The meeting was called to vote, by way of a qualified majority basis, on an issue of central concern: a proposal to limit the European working week to 48 hours. Naturally the plan was phrased in such a way as to allow for legitimate derogations ('exceptions to the rule') and to accommodate tolerable deviances but it was, nevertheless, an attempt to pass into European law a mandatory approach to regulating working practices in the twelve member states. This had never been done before and it would mark, therefore, a watershed in EU social legislation.

Hitherto, the passage of the Single European Act in 1986 with its commitment to some 300 ways of improving the workings of the Common Market had caused a degree of dissension in Britain. Such issues as the perceived bureaucratization of the EU and the increase in the EU budget – especially the spending on the Common Agricultural Policy – had raised some hackles. But there had been considerable support in political and industrial ranks for the legislation, since it opened up the European mainland and gave better access for British goods.

Britain's decision to join the Exchange Rate Mechanism (ERM), taken by prime minister Margaret Thatcher in 1990, was also seen as problematic by many. But not by the Conservative government who, until 16 September 1992, claimed that membership of the ERM was in Britain's fundamental interest since it kept imported inflationary pressures firmly at bay and forced British industrialists, who could not rely on a depreciating currency to sell their goods, to become much more efficient. Since Britain's unavoidable decision to quit the ERM on that day – forced because of massive speculation against the pound – the government has been obliged, conversely, to proclaim the virtues of a floating pound as being in the interests of British exporters.

Even today, opinion is divided on the merits of countries' either belonging to semi-fixed exchange rate clubs (which guarantee trading costs stability) or free-floating (which allows currencies' values to adjust continuously to traders' perceptions of economic prospects). There is, however, agreement that the rate at which Britain entered the ERM originally (DM2.95) was too high (and led to a highly overvalued pound) and that the relative level of the Deutschmark against other EU currencies over the period of German integration was also too high, since it resulted more from the high interest rates prevalent in Germany rather than from a true reflection of the country's economic prospects.

Both of these, in terms of their impact on employment conditions across Europe, have had, and are having, massive deflationary consequences. France, in particular and despite the turmoil of August 1993 in the exchange rate market, is now squeezed between a 'franc fort' policy and, like Britain and Italy, massive reductions in its budgetary deficit. The first is needed since membership of the ERM is an essential ingredient for economic and monetary union in the European Union; the second is imperative because of the economic consequences of a spiralling deficit. Table 1.2 indicates some of these major employment conditions differentials.

The Maastricht Treaty is another bone of contention between Britain and its mainland EU partners to the point where Prime Minister John Major was prepared to sign it only if Britain were given two 'opt-outs'. In the area of economics, the British were allowed to decide at some later stage whether they wished to opt for economic and monetary union (EMU) on the basis

Table 1.2 *Comparative working time and income data (mid-1993) for selected members*[6]

Country	Statutory maximum working time (Exc. overtime) (hours)	Days holiday per year (including national holidays)	Statutory minimum wage level (£/hour)	Typical pension as % of final average earnings claimed for a dependent spouse
Germany	48	42	4.70	69
France	39	35	3.40	88
Spain	40	38	1.20	89
Netherlands	48	41	3.80	38
UK	Nil	35	Nil	39

Table 1.3 *Comparative employment approaches*

Employment feature	France	Germany	UK
Minimum pay agreements	√	√	×
Maximum working hour agreement	√	√	×
Minimum holidays agreement	√	√	×
Statutory works council	√	√	×
Statutory board level employee representation	√	√	×

of a single currency and a federal bank. This involved not only membership of the ERM but also the ability to meet formidable convergence criteria on such performance ratios as government debt/GDP and budget deficit/GDP, considered by many commentators to be highly deflationary in themselves and hence to be potential unemployment raisers.

As we have seen, the second area in which Britain obtained an opt-out was on the Social Chapter of the Treaty. This was, in effect, a distillation of the measures which had been proposed over time by the European Commission, and endorsed especially by France and Germany to balance the claimed social interests of working people in Europe with the business advances represented by moves to create the Common Market.

The British government reckoned that the entire Social Charter edifice,[7] which was encapsulated in the Social Chapter and which ostensibly made for better worker protection and representation, was little more than a tax on business efficiency and was to be resisted at all costs. The disparity in approach between the UK and its two major European competitors can be seen in Table 1.3.

The watershed spoken of earlier in respect of the Luxembourg meeting relates to the application of aspects of the Social Charter in individual countries. The 48-hour working week directive represents, in effect, a sort of federal regulation. Its introduction, under the guidelines of policy on health and safety at work (as opposed to workers' rights) has meant that decision making in the Council of Ministers could be on a qualified majority – and not a unanimity – basis. As a consequence, Britain could not use its veto. The result of the meeting was an agreement by eleven EU members to endorse the plan to make a level playing field of working times and a statement of total opposition to the move by one member – Britain. David Hunt, Britain's employment minister, not only abstained from the vote but also announced that his government would challenge the result in the European Court of Justice as 'an abuse of treaty powers'. Its discussion as a health and safety matter was 'phoney'.[8]

A matter of economics

It is impossible to address the many issues that arise from a study of comparative management approaches in Europe without an awareness of the current economic situation. We have already touched on several of the key effects of the 1989–93 recession in the EU which shows signs of slow but sustained improvement. The challenges confronting Hoover, Sopalin, Timex and Grundig are not simply those of company owners seeking to sharpen company performance but of managers fighting for corporate survival in a hostile marketplace under adverse demand conditions. This section deals with just two of the economic problems whose consequences EU companies must deal with in handling their workforces. Each demands a substantial, and growing, volume of the resources that ultimately can only be provided through taxes on individual purchasing, earnings and wealth and on corporate profits.

The most salient issue facing the European Union in mid-1994 was the existence, nature and implications of large-scale unemployment. It was expected that the level of about 17.5 million out of work would have risen by the end of the year to 18 million. Compared with Japan and the USA, where 75 per cent and 70 per cent of people of working age had jobs, the EU was doing comparatively badly. Its score on this success dimension was 60 per cent.

The EU Commissioner for Social Affairs, Padraig Flynn, is charged with the responsibility of dealing with this problem in EU-wide terms by implementing a strategy which can be endorsed by the twelve EU members through their agreement on the size of the Community budget. The strategy, launched at the 1992 December summit, was focused clearly on an attempt to improve competitiveness against a background of a hoped-for breakthrough in the Uruguay Round of the GATT trade talks. These have had faltering progress – despite their universal appeal – because of the extent of protectionist views in the three competing trade blocs, Japan, the USA and the EU. Even after the GATT agreement in December 1993, they still face an uncertain future, so far as the EU is concerned, because of a difference in orientation among members of the need to protect the agricultural interest. In contrast, the other element in the background is more positive. This is the extension of the European Union of the twelve into the European Economic Area, through agreement on common market principles and practices with the Nordic and Alpine countries and their application for entry to the EU.

Describing the strategy for growth, Padraig Flynn's predecessor, Vasso Papandreou, declared:

> We have been trying to put the problem of unemployment back on the Community agenda for some months. The EC's Edinburgh summit in December 1992 approved an economic growth initiative. This is welcome but it does not go nearly far enough. It is also a pity that the summit did not agree a higher EC budget. That would have allowed more money to be spent on R&D, increasing the competitiveness of the European economy and leading to the creation of more jobs . . . We need some form of intervention to provide better training for our citizens. Allocating more financial resources to poorer parts of the Community does not help these areas alone. This has a multiplier effect.[9]

Britain was one of the countries to whom she referred as being hostile to the notions of increasing the EU budget and to the use of such increases for interventionist purposes. This should not surprise us, since the political complexion of the British government of the time was, in matters of economic and political philosophy, highly liberal, while Vasso Papandreou came from a solid Socialist background as a Greek politician.

The size of the political challenge posed by unemployment was indicated by a study carried out into the employment plans of the EU's top 100 companies.[10] Deputy Director Herbert Maier, commenting on the results, said that 'There is a real chance that unemployment in OECD countries will reach 34 million by the end of the decade'. While this figure seems over-exaggerated, if not alarmist, there is certainly a worrying lack of agreement about the action that is indicated to curb the rise in joblessness. For Maier, the migration of European jobs to Pacific Rim countries was a key issue.[10] Peter Spencer, chief economist for Kleinwort Benson, was of the opinion that the Social Chapter was beginning to look like a 'luxury that Europe could not afford', given that 'Europe has higher labour costs, very high social welfare costs and, if the GATT agreement goes ahead, it will no longer be able to rely as heavily on protectionism'.[10] Padraig Flynn himself saw the problem thus:

If some states pursue high standards of employment conditions while others deliberately seek short-term advantage by driving standards down, then the functioning of the Single market is threatened and pressures for returning economic policy to a national basis may become irresistible . . . Far from being a brake on the drive for growth and employment, progressive social measures are the *sine qua non* of economic success.

Europe's economic future lies not in a futile competition with the low-wage producers of the developing world, but in the knowledge-intensive industries of the next century. The social dimension is economically necessary because it is part of creating a level playing field for fair competition.[11]

July 1992 saw an appeal for 'a cooperative growth strategy for more employment' which echoed some aspects of this viewpoint. It was made jointly by the Union of Industrial and Employers Confederations (UNICE) and the European Trade Union Confederation (ETUC).[12] Spokesman Zygmunt Tyszkiewicz of UNICE listed the key conditions for success for this strategy as:

1 A guarantee of stability in the European business climate through a move towards economic and monetary union, as specified in the Maastricht accord.
2 A rise in confidence from the resolute completion of the single market and its extension to the EFTA countries.
3 An improvement in the macro-economic climate to be achieved by reduction in budget deficits (through lower government expenditures), without eating into public investment and without relaxing monetary policy. This would allow the necessary reduction in interest rates (reducing wage pressures) and restore the 'virtuous circle' of growth, job creation and investment in a climate of stable prices.
4 An improvement in the EU skills base.

He also stressed the extent to which permissive collective agreements – work contracts, shift systems, recruitment and dismissal laws – could be counterproductive in exceeding their legitimate ends of giving protection to workers. Wage structures should, he argued, reflect productivity differences and not be distorted by minimum wage thinking. Finally, the strategy called for a review of fiscal and social security legislation to reduce non-labour costs. The relationship between minimum wage and other economic performance data can be observed in Table 1.5.

The issue of productivity was, and is, critical to the possibility of revitalizing the EU economy. Analysis by the Confederation of British Industry shows that EU manufacturing productivity growth rates over the 1980s lagged 2 percentage points behind Japan and 1 percentage point behind the

Table 1.5 *Selected economic performance data*[13]

Country	Minimum official wage level £/hour 1991 (1)	Corporate profit tax: 1992 (%) (2)	Typical 1992 pension as % of final earnings (3)	Overall world competitiveness rank (4)
UK	–	33	39	17
France	3.40	34	70	14
Germany	4.30	50	56	2

Table 1.6 *The ageing problem (Eurostat data)*

Country	Inhabitants aged 65+ (millions) 1990	2040	Anticipated growth in population size (millions)	% of total growth	Cumulative growth (%)
France	7.66	12.74	5.08	26.2	
Spain	5.05	9.23	4.18	21.6	47.8
Italy	7.89	11.67	3.78	19.5	67.3
UK	8.54	11.78	3.24	16.7	84.0
Germany	9.46	12.50	3.04	15.7	100.0
Total	38.60	57.92	19.32	100	

USA. The gap is expected to increase rather than decrease in the 1990s.[2] So is that of growth. The Union's share of world trade had fallen since 1980 by 20 per cent and imports were rising rapidly. According to the Commission the EU would require a steady growth of 2.5 per cent per year to service its current unemployment level. It was hoped that the GATT agreement signed in December 1993 would help this materially.

Economic growth would be also needed to deal with Europe's second key challenge: demographic change. Analysis shows that, at the start of the 1990s, one European in fifteen was over the age of seventy-five and that, by the turn of the century, the level would be fully 10 per cent. A more detailed picture of the problem is given in Table 1.6. The existence of significant differences between EU members' pension fund schemes, their eligibility criteria and entitlement to benefits indicated that harmonization of systems would not be feasible in anything like the near future.[14] This added considerable spice to the discussion of how pensions – as well as unemployment benefits – would, in fact, be funded, in the event that the economic performance of the European Union did not improve.

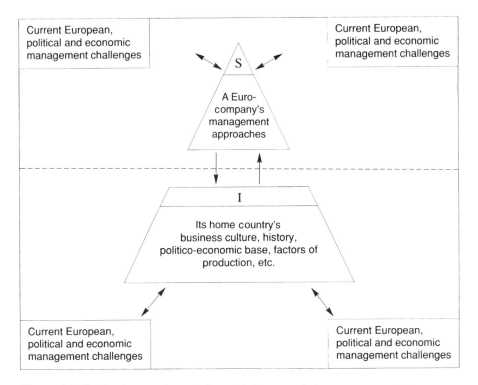

Figure 1.1 The business culture iceberg. A framework for reviewing differences in countries' managerial approaches. S = superstructural factors (the visible part of the business culture iceberg); I = infrastructural factors (the invisible part). ⟶ Influences, determinants, shapers; – – – – the dividing line between the cultural aspects we can easily see and those that act as invisible shapers

Managing people: organizational aspects

Having outlined some of the key political and economic issues which frame, at least in part, the decision space of top managers in trans-European firms, we can now turn our attention to some of the organizational matters that are of primary concern. The position of these is shown in Figure 1.1. This serves as a basic framework with which we can explore the subject of managing people across Europe. It should be noted that the iceberg framework has been arbitrarily chosen for illustrative purposes and for its simplicity.

Here, the functional activities involved in managing people – hiring, firing, paying, training, motivating, organizing and the use of appropriate management styles – are seen as superstructural activities which are inter-dependent with infrastructural aspects of political and societal management. The latter arise from elements in a nation's history, its factors of production and politico-economic base and the way in which all three of these have shaped, and are shaping, the nation's business culture. A salient conclusion from this book is that the infrastructural aspects of British management differ so extensively from their mainland European counterparts as to constitute a separate paradigm or model. In contrast, many of the technical activities in the superstructure are identical, or almost so, across the entire European spectrum. This section deals with two of the infrastructural aspects thought to be of key significance: the question of (1) organizational partnership and (2) organizational change.

Continental Europe has an approach to management of people – their pay, their working contracts, recruitment and termination practices – that is characterized by the concept of partnership between the owners of the company, its management, its unions and workforce. This is not necessarily manifested in the visibility of the personnel department, although some 70–80 per cent of Spanish and French firms do have a human resources board director and represent the highest level of personnel interests. Nor are some human resource departments focused on issues in the round, as opposed to one specific aspect. Indeed, the attention of personnel managers in unionized firms in Italy is predominantly with industrial relations. Where the partnership notion does come to the fore is in the areas of consultation with the workforce and its representatives on matters of strategic – and not just technical management – importance to the firm, as in the case of the typical Japanese firm in the EU. These can include such matters as the creation of a social plan (France), joint agreement on training schemes and policies for recruitment and termination (Spain, Italy). As we shall see later, this partnership comes strongly to the fore in the deliberations of works councils (e.g. French comité d'entreprise).

According to Chris Brewster and Ariane Hegewisch,[15] one general tendency in Europe has been, and increasingly is, for speedy movement on the part of firms towards greater flexibility in bargaining structures. The switch is away from national, pan-industry settlements towards individual company or plant-based agreements and is accompanied, typically, by devolvement of pay-setting from personnel specialists to line managers. However, the pace is noticeably slower in Germany and the Netherlands, countries where the notion of partnership is especially strong, than in France, Spain and the UK. In fact, it is in the UK that the idea of performance-related pay has the strongest appeal.[16]

Another tendency noted by Brewster and Hegewisch is the move by firms towards more flexible working. This has been accelerated by the demands for labour economy brought on by the recession over the period 1989–93 and by the increasing impact of new technology. All sectors of the

European economy and all countries have been affected by the assimilation
of such innovations as temporary or fixed-term contracts and increasing
part-time work. Again the Continental experience is one of discussion among
the social partners prior to the take-up of such schemes.

Exhibit 1.1 *Re-engineering by numbers*[17]

'Re-engineering is ... the fundamental re-thinking and radical re-design of
business processes to achieve organizational results in critical, contemporary
measures of performance such as cost, quality, service and speed. At present
everyone involved in a process (in "functional silos" like Marketing or Finance)
looks inward towards their department and upward toward their boss but
no-one looks outward toward the customer.'

Not that this implies a cosy relationship between, say, French and German unions and managers. The recent experience of the IG Metall strike in
Germany indicates to the contrary, but even here the dissension was still
handled within a highly structured discussion framework which was the
product of over two decades of participative management.

Organizational change is the second issue. The British Institute of Management report *The Flat Organization – Philosophy and Practice*, issued in 1991,
contained the results of an interesting survey of British firms and their
approaches to managing organizational change. Respondents indicated that
they were becoming organizationally slimmer and flatter (88 per cent), undertaking more through teamwork (79 per cent) and increasing the company's responsiveness (78 per cent) through better networking and greater
inter-dependence of functions (71 per cent). For the majority, centralized,
bureaucratic, top-down order-giving was being replaced by network and
team-based organizations (project groups, multi-functional teams, etc.). The
influence of the Japanese thrust towards total quality management (TQM)
and just-in-time (JIT) was noticeable.

There was also a trend towards the 'virtual corporation'. This is a form
of corporate organization which buys in from external partners all the services it needs (including manufacturing) rather than 'owning' them (less
economically) in-house. It can source these services literally from anywhere
provided it is able to sell the finished product, however and wherever
made, in the markets of its choice. This is the facility that underlies what the
French call the strategy of de-localization to which we will refer later.

This trend is not surprising in the light of the recent impressive flood
from the USA of literature on organization change. In the period from Tom
Peter's *Thriving on Chaos* (1987) to his *Liberation Management* (1993) there
has been an outpouring of exhortations on changing the organizational

architecture, business process redesign, organizational re-engineering etc. The names of Senge (*The Fifth Discipline*, 1991) and Kotter and Heskett (*Corporate Culture and Performance*, 1992) are prominent in the change agent field. Such advice does not find as ready an acceptance in mainland Europe, where, again, the notion of partnership precludes the treatment of the workforce as factors of production – to be rearranged at will.

Three frictions on the process of change are of interest, here. First, there is the extent to which termination of work is especially difficult in Holland and Belgium. In some cases the approval of the works council is needed before management can take action. Certainly, specific reasons must be given. Second is the challenge involved in job changing. Until relatively recently executive search was illegal in Germany and it is still not fully accepted in Denmark. To change one's job in Germany involves the supply to one's prospective employer of *Zeugnisse* (written reports attesting one's capabilities) from one's existing employer. Third, there is the question of the strategic intervention of the European Union's Court of Justice in employment matters, most recently in 1990. Then the landmark Barber case laid down that the principle of equal treatment for men and women did apply to pensions.

Elements of business culture

As explained in Figure 1.1, the organizational factors of European management are seen as heavily dependent on (and themselves heavily influencing) the business culture of particular nations. Here, this is taken to be not so much the anthropological–sociological elements involved in the business structures and socialization process (analysed by Hofstede, see Table 1.7), who concluded that much of management was culture-bound, so much as the way the nation's history, geography, factors of production, politics and economics have shaped 'how things are done round here'.

To illustrate the extent to which these factors affect the way in which people are managed across Europe, it is useful to refer to the brief historical overview of Britain, France and Germany given in the Appendix to this chapter.[19]

The key elements of the business culture infrastructure of the three countries which are of importance to the economist clearly are:

1 The extent to which their factors of production (location, physical– human–financial resources) differ from country to country.
2 The extent to which their economies differ in terms of their category contributions (e.g. manufacture of goods, agriculture, supply of services, entrepôt activity, rentier yield) and, within the manufacturing sector, the comparative strength of light and heavy manufacturing.

Table 1.7 *Hofstede's four dimensions of culture*[18]

Dimension of culture analysed by Hofstede	Commentary
Individualism/collectivism	Concerned with nature of relationships between a person as an individual and his or her fellow human beings. Individualism signifies that the ties are very loose. Collectivism exists in societies where people tend to look after each other and social groups are of primary importance.
Power distance	Those societies which are interested in egalitarianism tend to try to reduce (or play down) the inequalities of power and wealth. Hofstede called them low-power distance cultures. High-power distance cultures are those that tolerate/maintain/increase those inequalities.
Uncertainty avoidance	Countries which have rules and regulations and other organizational procedures to deal with uncertainty are called strong uncertainty-avoidance societies. Here, management approaches tend to revolve around tasks, systems, discipline and goals.
Masculinity/femininity	A masculine society is one which distinguishes very clearly in its role allocations by sex the jobs to be done by men and by women. In a masculine society, the hero is typically a superman. A feminine society typically involves cooperation, tolerance and plays down sex-role divisions.

3 The extent to which their economies differ in the level of automation and labour intensity (the human/machine balance), productivity and competitiveness levels.

4 The extent of a country's welfare state and the flexibility or otherwise of its system for disbursing benefits.

Our interest, however, lies predominantly in the extent to which companies in these three countries are managed. We shall concentrate on aspects of two factors: comparing and contrasting the nature of the ownership of firms and the nature of the relationship between companies and commercial banks.

Figure 1.2 illustrates a trade-off between types of political governance and economic management of a nation's affairs. Using this analytical framework

**Form of
political
governance**

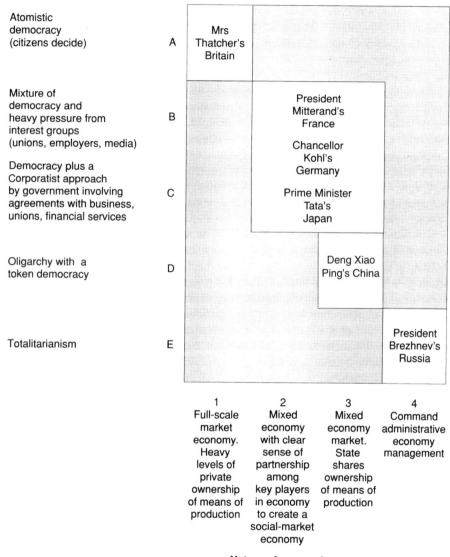

Atomistic
democracy
(citizens decide)   A

Mixture of
democracy and
heavy pressure from   B
interest groups
(unions, employers, media)

Democracy plus a
Corporatist approach
by government involving   C
agreements with business,
unions, financial services

Oligarchy with a
token democracy   D

Totalitarianism   E

Mrs
Thatcher's
Britain

President
Mitterand's
France

Chancellor
Kohl's
Germany

Prime Minister
Tata's
Japan

Deng Xiao
Ping's China

President
Brezhnev's
Russia

1	2	3	4
Full-scale market economy. Heavy levels of private ownership of means of production	Mixed economy with clear sense of partnership among key players in economy to create a social-market economy	Mixed economy market. State shares ownership of means of production	Command administrative economy management

Nature of economic management

Figure 1.2 A typology of political economies.

and the earlier historical data we can place each country in a relevant position on the matrix.

Britain, under Mrs Thatcher and, later, John Major, has lived through a long period of privatization in which the main state-owned enterprises were progressively sold off. This had the benefits of destroying state monopolies – in all cases actual competitors were created to challenge the old monopolies – and providing the Conservative government with the money needed to keep the public deficit lower than it would otherwise have been. The expansion in the public ownership of shares allowed government to make increasing claims for the political attractiveness of popular capitalism. Private, rather than public, ownership of sold-off companies in competitive conditions kept prices down. The numbers in employment in what had been state enterprises fell, thus bringing down the cost of operation. Coupled with effective strategic action against the trade unions (legislation in 1980, 1982 and 1984), which significantly reduced their powers and their authority, workforces all over Britain were more amenable to accepting new technology and, increasingly, becoming more cost-competitive.

But the industrial base continued to be eroded by highly competitive imports, on the one hand, and the existence of high-quality, low-cost manufacturing centres outside the UK which could be used as a substitute, on the other. No limits were placed by the UK government on manufacturers' freedom to export capital and manufacture overseas, just as none were set on any in-bound investment by Japanese or US companies who were seeking a high-quality, low-cost manufacturing centre within Europe. Indeed, quite the converse happened. This was needed by some Japanese companies to guarantee them access to the EU marketplace in the event of a breakdown in the GATT trade talks.

These considerations place 1990s Britain in quadrant A-1 in Figure 1.2. Currently, trade unions have no share in political authority and very little, if any, access to political power-sharing. Big business and, in particular, the City of London are dominant forces in the economic spectrum but even here their powers are limited by the de-regulation of the financial services marketplace and by the care with which British politicians maintain the separation of powers in political and commercial life. Market economics are seen as the sure route forward by the current government and state intervention in commercial and industrial matters is seen as both unwise and unnecessary.

France and Germany have a different shape to their democratic system. Instead of the British 'first-past-the-post' electoral system, elements of proportional representation are used. This has the effect of producing governments that reflect the spread of votes to a greater degree. In the case of Germany, the result has been a degree of centrist political stability which has paralleled the nation's self-reinforcing industrial structure arrangements among its companies, unions and banks and aided the relationship between government and business. The political majority enjoyed by the

Conservative government in Britain since 1979 has been less due to the nature of the electoral system, which, if anything, makes for divisiveness and intermittent instability of a kind unwelcome to business executives, than to the weaknesses of the opposition parties and the perceived attractiveness of the Conservative ideology during this period. Over a similar period French governments have oscillated wildly, especially as regards nationalization/ privatization of state enterprise. The current French Balladur programme is aimed at reducing the extent of French state ownership of the commanding heights of the economy, but whether it will alter in any way the entrenched cross-ownership systems of key French firms is anyone's guess.

It needs to be well understood that the French and German governments and their nations' businesses, whether private or state-owned, are strongly averse to foreign ownership and control. Their patterns of ownership and commercial bank support are such as to deter attack, and it is this security which allows the management of these firms to develop strategic vision and plans which are often beyond the reach of the short-termist British. The latter's commercial performance is dictated less by the strategic requirements of customers than by the pattern of profitability likely in the next few years.

Such patterns of ownership, coupled with the relatively high social benefits and wages of the French and the Germans and the settled, constitution-framed nature of their highly bureaucratic administrations, have created a politico-economic system whose industrial elements, though seemingly more durable and predictable than Britain's, are arguably neither as adjustable nor as efficient. Under these conditions it is not inappropriate (though populist) to label the British style of industrial management as that of a 'Robin Hood' approach: quick to react, easy to innovate, responsive, commercially-driven. 'The Sheriff of Nottingham' model – systematic, all-embracing, tightly controlled, centrist, standardized – tends also to fit many aspects of German and French corporatism. Each has its merits and disadvantages.

Protection of ownership may be a more secure way of maintaining one's own indigenous industry than protection through tariff barriers and quotas. By analogy, it will be recalled that the state-appointed sheriff had legal title to the forest as well as command of the administration and no shortage of resources with which to grind down his opponent. Robin Hood's approach was not appropriate for the long haul.

But, as maintained above, in the Europe of the 1990s the security of corporatist protectionism (if, in fact, 'real') is not necessarily beneficial, in a macro- or even micro-economic sense, to those who seek to apply it. The freedom of manoeuvre of the French and German economies is much less than that of the British. They have all the stakeholder pressures surrounding them and weighty and inflexible governmental machinery systems propelling them forwards to possibly an even higher unit cost future than their already costly present.

The German car industry is an excellent example of the problems of management that are now arising. By comparison with Japanese plants undeniably it was overmanned and undermodernized. Critics assert that it still suffers from overgenerous working practices. 'Foreign investors are making a grand detour around Germany simply because our costs are simply too high' says Peter Blum of the Deutsche Industrie und Handelstag.[20] Expansion of this industry is taking place in central Europe, not in Germany.

The present state of play in the German unions is another example. They have been engaged in crucial bargaining on a new social compact with government and management to restore competitiveness to Germany's $2 trillion economy, yet one leading union – IG Metall – had no hesitation in early 1993 in calling 70 000 East German members out on strike to support a claim for 26 per cent wage rises. Admittedly, this had been promised previously by management, yet the very idea makes impossible the view that comparatively low labour costs in the former East Germany would lead that region out of its Communist legacy of economic decline.

Yet another problem would arise if the Deutsche Bank set an example for other German leading banks – as it has said it might – by selling off some of its holdings in industrial Germany, for example part of the 28.2 per cent of Daimler-Benz it owns. This would be a move of immense significance. According to commentator Allen Saunderson,

> share ownership lies at the heart of the country's universal banking system
> ... which is more secure than in the USA or Britain where such cross-holdings
> are forbidden ... The system also allows German banks to work closely with
> industry by providing ... a reliable long-term source of capital to underpin
> industrial expansion.[21]

For France, the problems confronting the Balladur administration are twofold: how to break with the *dirigisme* of the recent Socialist government and how to square the circle of allowing free international competition, within GATT, and still protecting vulnerable strategic parts of French industry, such as computers and agriculture. The problems lie in the fact of the large-scale expansion in French unemployment that could follow either or both methods.

Of the two, de-localization (or in Anglo-Saxon, globalization) is the more feared. There has been a substantial fall in French employment (as in Britain) resulting from the exporting of French manufacturing capacity to lower-cost locations. The Arthuis report which went to government at the beginning of May 1993 stated that protectionism might have to be considered to address a situation where non-OECD country exports (i.e. from newly industrializing and exporting countries) rose from 9.2 per cent of total EU imports to 13.7 per cent in 1992.[22] Since then France has signed the GATT accord, reducing her tariff base considerably.

For these reasons, the position of the French and Germans in Figure 1.2 lies in quadrants B/C–2/3. This is fully in accord with the Maastricht stance taken by both countries. The problem is that to improve competitiveness, steps need to be taken to follow the example of Britain (moving from the existing quadrant reference to a position more like Britain's: A-1), rather than reinforce the very kernel of uncompetitiveness that is seen to lie (in British eyes), for the very best of social policy reasons, in the Social Charter. This paradox is one of the factors which may reveal the case of Hoover as a vitally important indicator of the fate of the European Union as manufacturer and trader.

Appendix: historical overview

Britain

Britain was, with France, the first industrialized country in Europe. It was early able to serve its growing Empire with goods (restricting access to colonies by the Navigation Acts to only British ships) and, through this protected trade advantage over its neighbours, was able to capitalize on further growth in its colonies to become an industrial power of the first rank.

The initial policy of mercantilism was replaced from the latter part of the eighteenth century onwards by a thrust, of greater or minor proportions, towards free trade coupled with imperial preference and then an unrestricted trading policy. This now involves an 'open door' to imports, whether of goods or investment capital, from whatever source.

Britain has remained an industrial leader, although, unconquered in war (unlike France, Germany and Japan), it has never had to re-equip industry with new technologies and plant as a direct result of defeat. But Britain has lost ground to more dynamic competitors in low added-value and high-tech, mass-production industries. This has been due in the latter stage of the twentieth century in part to management–labour rigidities and, in part, to a comparative lack of capital investment.

The British system of private and commercial banking that developed out of the needs of a colonial empire and the attendant industrialization was concerned with creating wealth, first and foremost. It seemed to focus on building industry as a by-product of this aim, always lending funds at interest rather than (as in France and Germany) buying shares in firms. Where funds were lent long-term, property was the preferred sector; where funds were lent to industry, short-term controls over corporate achievements were never far away.

Socio-politically, Britain also moved at a different pace from its Continental neighbours. Management of empire and the medieval guild system of industrial ownership and administration simply did not fit together from as early as the sixteenth century. The guild system died, and with it the concept of a state-regulated workforce management system. Industry became politicized early, with trade unions achieving recognition in 1824 in England (1884 in France).

The system in Britain at the turn of the twenty-first century is orientated towards *laissez-faire*. Indeed, under the prime ministership of Margaret Thatcher it received a major push in this direction. The Conservative government in the 1980s was enthusiastic about free trade, liberal in its economics, non-interventionist in its industrial policy and determined in its views that the requisite relationship between owners, company management and the trade unions should involve a significant productivity improvement and the maximum possible factor freedom. The opposition of the Conservative government to Social Charter aspects of European union (working week, retirement age, pensions, Sunday rest day, maternity leave) at the start of the 1990s hinged on such views. Unit labour costs are commensurately low.

It is worth noting that the break with the Church of Rome (under Henry VIII) and the rise of Protestantism in England created the foundation for a financial services industry which was a major strategic weapon in Britain's empire building. The strictures of the Catholic church against usury (from Gration in the twelfth century onwards) greatly inhibited the creation of banking and finance systems in Catholic countries and held back the sort of popular bourgeois commercialism which rapidly expanded in Britain from the fourteenth century onwards.

A 1991 report issued by the Confederation of British Industry (*Competing with the World's Best*) was highly critical of the extent to which British industry, financial institutions and the civil service are 'unusually fragmented' and claims that the Treasury and the Bank of England have 'an insufficient depth of understanding about the realities of manufacturing'. On this, John Banham (Director-General of the CBI) commented that it was an opportunity for the government to look beyond 'the short-term requirements of its domestic economics' to 'the strategic positioning of our manufacturing industries in global markets' in the next century.

France

France was industrialized before Germany. The initial pattern of state backing for industry and commerce under Jean Baptiste Colbert, Minister of Finance under Louis XIV, was entrenched within the overarching ideology of mercantilism: the concept that the business of the state was to amass

Table 1.8 *Shifts in the make-up of the French economy (1980–91)*[23]

Branches of the economy	% of total employed		% of total value added	
	1980	1991	1980	1991
Agriculture	8.6	5.7	4.5	3.2
Industry	34.3	28.2	35.5	29.9
Services	57.1	66.1	60.0	66.9
Total	100	100	100	100

Note that the French budget deficit was forecast to reach 4.8 per cent of the GDP in 1993 and the deficit on the Social Fund would reach 60.2 billion francs, some 35 billion up on 1992.

wealth. This pattern fitted in well with a hierarchical social system, family ownership and a legacy of guild discipline until the revolutionary changes of the late eighteenth century. It was the case, however, that France lost out in its mercantilist rivalry – maritime and colonial – with England.

The system's ability to adapt and meet the requirements of war was tested to the limit under Napoleon I, who produced for his European empire the formula of external protection – through the Continental System – and internal industrial revitalization to meet the needs of war. This took place through, for example, the setting up of chambers of commerce (1801) as an aid to commerce and conciliation boards (*Conseils de Prud'hommes*) to deal with labour problems. Such institutions helped to carry forward the concept of the need for commercial and industrial training, an idea that had been supported by guilds until they were abolished in 1774. Napoleon's reforms also included the creation of a powerful, skilled and meritocratic state bureaucracy (based on the *grandes écoles*) which has endured.

The need for French banks to assist in industrial development as a matter of principle was well established under Napoleon II, who set up Crédit Foncier and Crédit Mobilier specifically for this purpose. Conversely, the French state's involvement in industrial and commercial ownership and management is very much a post-1945 phenomenon (see Table 1.8). The Tenth National Plan covered the period 1989–92 and laid down indicative targets and broad policy thrusts. But here, too, policy has oscillated, depending on economic circumstances. The prevailing mood of the socialist government in France in the early 1990s was for a retrenchment of the ownership and control which had been painstakingly built up – through the policy of developing 'national champion' firms – in the late 1980s. For this the services of nationalized banks had been used in no small measure. The 'Ni Ni' approach of President Mitterand (no more nationalization, no more privatization) is now at an end. The victory of the right under the leadership of prime minister Edouard Balladur is set to usher in a policy of mammoth privatization of state enterprise. Worker consultation, through the *comité d'entreprise* (works committee) system, is carried out in all firms employing 50 people or more.

Germany

The Industrial Revolution came late to Germany. Only after 1860 did it become a marked feature, and then with quickly increasing clarity. Previously, the country had a history of localized manufacture, innumerable tariff barriers, bad roads and little capital – all expressive of the political fragmentation that existed among the innumerable German states prior to Bismarck and the (predominantly European and land-based) German Empire in the nineteenth century.

Limited partnerships in, and family ownership of, manufacturing firms were common whereas limited companies, unlike in England, were a comparative rarity until the latter part of the century. A key further impetus to industrialization within the authoritarian Empire under Bismarck came in 1870, with Germany's devastating victory over the French in the Franco-Prussian War. To assist with improving the manufacturing base, the Deutsche and Dresdner banks were set up in 1870 and 1872, respectively, the previous banking structure under the farming cooperative Raffeisen banks being wholly inadequate to the task of promoting industrial growth.

From this date, it was cooperation (through loans) between the German banking and industry systems and then, increasingly, co-ownership (through equity holdings) which can be seen to have contributed to Germany's success as an *Industriestaat*. Over a period in excess of a century – interrupted by defeats in two world wars and by Hitler's totalitarian dictatorship – this form of banking–industry complex has safeguarded German industrial ownership. The latter has itself been safeguarded by the possibility of applying the shareholder voting law or *Stimmrecht* (in which voting rights do not depend on share ownership level), as well as promoting its development. State ownership of industry in Germany is, by contrast, not a particularly prominent feature: aid for R&D is.

One by-product of the need to develop and protect was the early creation in Germany of giant enterprises, spanning a huge range of activities within a particular industry, such as the early *Kartells* (nineteenth century) and the *Konzerne* (like Krupp and IG Farben), in the twentieth. Present-day examples are Siemens and Daimler-Benz, in which Deutsche Bank has a 28 per cent stake, which could well be called *Kombinate*. With cross-ownerships and the safeguard of the *Mitbestimmung* principle (worker co-determination via worker membership of supervisory boards), such firms are well-nigh impregnable to predatory attack. Workers in them enjoy substantial statutory employment rights (working time, representation, training, maternity leave, job protection, etc.), a factor which makes for a high level of commitment of maintenance of the status quo – as well as very high labour costs. Interestingly, some of the features of the current *Gewerkkammer* statutory training and employment regulations date back to the medieval guild system, which was, in fact, never abolished in Germany. Indeed, in the nineteenth century, several of its institutions became instruments for state insurance as well as training.

References

1 Bremner, C., 'Hoover jobs sweep away Mitterrand hopes for elections', *The Times*, 30 January 1993.
2 Walker, L., 'Delors counts the cost of war on jobs', *The European*, 27–30 May 1993.
3 'Sopalin: le choc de deux cultures', *Le Monde*, 27 April 1993.
4 'Fin du conflit à l'usine Kimberly–Clark–Sopalin', *Le Monde*, 9/10 May 1993.
5 'Michelin annonce la suppression de 2950 emplois', *Le Monde*, 9/10 May 1993.
6 (a) Datastream W. Cologne, Bacon and Woodraw, Noble Lowndes. (b) Eurostat, Woodrow Milliman. 'Northerners lose out in final years', *The European*, 8–11 April 1993.
7 The Community Charter of Fundamental Social Rights for Workers, Commission of the European Community, May 1990.
8 Brock, G., 'UK goes to court over EC working week vote', *The Times*, 2 June 1993.
9 'Papandreou, V., 'Spread wealth to create more opportunity', *The European*, 30 December 1992–3 January 1993.
10 Wassell, T. and Castle, T., '8 million to join the workless force', *The European*, 31 December 1992–3 January 1993.
11 'Ill-tempered struggle for a "Social Europe" ', *The European* 4–7 March 1993.
12 Gabaglio, E., 'Knocking on doors to boost recovery', *The European*, 30 December 1992–3 January 1993.
13 (a) Income Data Services, European Report. (b) KPMG. (c) Woodrow Milliman, Noble Lowndes. (d) World Competitiveness Report.
14 'Pensions time bomb', *The European* 8–11 April 1993.
15 Brewster, C. and Hegewisch, A., 'A continent of diversity', *Personnel Management*, January 1993.
16 *Sunday Times*, 11 April 1993.
17 Hammer, M. and Champy, J., *Re-engineering the Corporation*, Harper Business, New York, 1993.
18 Hofstede, G., *'Culture's Consequences': International differences in work-related values*, Sage, Beverley Hills, 1980.

19 Garrison, T., *European Business Strategy*, 3rd edn, Elm Publications, Huntingdon, 1993.
20 'Germany in fear of social dumping', *The European*, 4–7 March 1993.
21 Saunderson, A., 'German bankers shake their industrial chains', *The European*, 25–28 March 1993.
22 Angel, P. and Monnot, C., 'Les delocalisations sont destructrices d'emplois', *Le Monde* 4 June 1993.
23 *Le Monde*, 18 May 1993.

2 Managing people in the United Kingdom

Shaun Tyson

Human resource management in the United Kingdom has undergone a quiet revolution. The term 'human resource management' itself signifies new priorities, and new approaches to the management of the employment relationship. However, this new order is rooted in the past traditions from which personnel management and its latest variant, human resource management, have sprung.

The traditions in personnel management

The origins of personnel management can be traced back to the work of the early welfare workers whose task at the turn of the century was to try to ameliorate, for those employers who had a conscience, some of the worst effects of *laissez-faire* capitalism. The industrialization of the UK had grown through coal mining, iron production and the application of steam power during the first part of the nineteenth century. It was the widespread adoption of Adam Smith's principles of the division of labour, the specialization and concentration into factories, and technological advances (for example, in steel manufacture) that brought large-scale production, wealth to the owners and a new urban working class. Some of the social implications of the new mode of production were the growth of towns such as Manchester and Birmingham and a rising working class comprising artisans, tradespeople, shopkeepers, clerks as well as new occupations, including engine drivers, civil engineers, tool makers and specialists in the many forms of manufacturing. Between 1850 and 1875 railways and shipping expanded nearly ten times, coal and iron production doubled and the system of manufacture moved towards mass production. This was all accompanied by a massive increase in population of 27 per cent between 1851 and 1871.[1, 2]

The effects of these changes were revolutionary. The slum squalor in the new towns, where people packed in to find work, produced appalling public health problems. Child labour and the long hours and low wages for the majority of working people, poor food and the lack of sanitation were among the conditions in which a few enlightened employers began to see the need for employee welfare.[3]

At the same time, the 'industrial betterment' movement began towards the end of the nineteenth century to improve living and working conditions. This movement found its expression through municipal actions to clear the slums and improve sanitation. Early welfare workers originated as 'Lady Bountifuls' who, although not employed themselves, acted on behalf of employers to visit the sick and to keep an eye on the physical as well as the moral welfare of women factory workers. The Quaker employers in particular, Rowntree, Cadbury and those who shared strong Christian beliefs, were seeking ways to overcome the conflict they experienced when earning profits from employing people on low wages.[4] 'Model' factories and 'model' villages such as the experiment by the Lever Brothers at Port Sunlight were attempts to show that it was possible for working people to live decently, while working within an efficient, profitable company.

By 1913 there was a sufficient number of welfare workers to form an association known as the Welfare Workers' Association, which was the forerunner to the Institute of Personnel Management.[5] Welfare concerns for boys and all employees were given a boost following the creation of the Industrial Society during the First World War and the increasing role of the state which had extended the franchise to working men was now, through safety legislation and the introduction of some minimum standards, beginning to lay the foundations for what could be seen as a more normative approach to managing people.[6] The notion that high productivity and welfare are related comes from the belief that motivation to work is a product of the treatment employees receive. This essentially unitary frame of reference derives from a belief in reciprocity, and is a paternalistic vision. Modern companies such as Marks & Spencer strongly follow this tradition where beliefs about people are acted out through personnel policies geared to the needs of individual employees.[7]

In contrast, the industrial relations tradition is based on a collectivist approach to the resolution of work problems. Trade unions in the United Kingdom have existed since at least the eighteenth century. The old 'guilds' were not the forerunners of unions, rather they were the original employers' associations. In medieval times guilds provided a sense of order, a system of training and material support to craftsmen, all of whom were masters in their own right. They were responsible for their apprentices who could eventually qualify as journeymen and as masters also.

The early trade unions were unions of craftspeople who banded together to negotiate their pay rates, to control entry to the craft and to maintain standards. In the building industry, stonemasons, carpenters and plumbers, for example, all belonged to different trade unions who would agree the rate for the job with their prospective employer before working on the building, much as they do today. Unions were important providers of friendly society benefits, helping members who were ill or unemployed.

There were no uniform pay rates or working hours. Unions began on a local scale, but national organization began in the mid-nineteenth century with engineers, iron founders, boilermakers, carpenters and joiners forming amalgamated societies out of local unions which maintained local autonomy in custom and practice, while providing minimum benefits to members and a basic set of rules governing hours and pay rates. The 'tramping' system allowed craftsmen to move about the country seeking work, and to receive modest financial relief at the 'houses of call' (often inns) according to an agreed system, controlled from the union offices. This was a way of dealing with local unemployment and of relieving local union branches of burdens, for example, during a strike.[8]

Trades councils developed in the towns from the 1850s, representing all trades in one district, and provided a forum for ideas on trade unions to spread. However, until the 1880s there were mostly small unions with a fluctuating membership dependent upon the trade cycle.[8] Early attempts to form trade unions suffered from repression by employers and by governments. In the early part of the nineteenth century trade unions were seen as subversive organizations by governments which used the Combination Acts to prevent unions from operating. It was not until 1871 that unions were declared safe from prosecution as criminal conspiracies for being 'in restraint of trade'. In 1875 peaceful picketing and strike action were permitted, and breach of contract was made a purely civil rather than a criminal matter.

Trade unions' legal rights have been the subject of continuous political influence throughout this century. In 1901 the Taff Vale judgment was a further setback for trade unionism because, as a consequence of this case, trade unions could be sued in the courts to obtain damages for the actions of their officials during disputes. The 1906 Act was therefore brought in by the Liberal government to reverse the effects of this judgment. The 1906 Act gave trade unions and their officials immunity from any claim for damages caused by actions in furtherance of a trade dispute. From these cases and others concerning, for example, picketing, political strikes and the political levy paid by trade union members to the Labour Party has come a feeling that the unions are struggling against the Establishment for their very existence. Such a notion is not implausible now, given the express intention of the 1979 Conservative government to reduce trade union power by limiting their legal protection.

One could argue that the nature and scope of trade unionism changed during the period from the 1880s to 1926. The end of the nineteenth century saw the rise of the unskilled unions, representing gas workers, dockers, transport workers and those in various semi-skilled factory occupations. Unlike the craft unions which had espoused the middle-class ideology of thrift, hard work and a support for the capitalist system, militants within the unskilled unions were more interested in widescale social reform and helped to found the Labour Party to pursue their political aims. These were not necessarily revolutionary, but were concerned with a radical shift in the distribution of wealth. The movement towards welfare benefits, with increased state expenditure and protection for workers' rights before the First World War, should be seen in the context of the rising tide of socialist opinion. The political aims of organized labour perhaps reached their strongest expression in the resistance to wage cuts which brought on the General Strike of 1926. After this there were few attempts to seize the political initiative by the labour movement as a whole.

During both world wars the government of the day had sought to come to agreements with the unions over the changes to working practices necessitated by wartime production.[6] The introduction of arbitration to avoid disputes and research into such issues as fatigue and ergonomics were also stimulated by wartime pressures to improve productivity. Until after the Second World War trade unions in the major industries negotiated with the appropriate employers' associations often in joint committees representing the unions in that particular industry. Such associations as the Engineering Employers' Federation constructed procedure agreements to cover disputes and monitored payment systems and the conditions of service offered by their member employers. During the last two decades there has been a shift towards plant- or company-level bargaining. Initially, this was occasioned by the need for productivity deals which could only be struck at the company or unit level, but pay controls have caused more activity at company level whenever prices and incomes policies were imposed.

By the 1960s, commentators were frequently blaming Britain's poor economic performance on trade union militancy and weak management. Specialists in the field of industrial relations were still relatively rare on the management side. Most major negotiations were undertaken by senior line managers. The pressure to settle and to maintain harmony by passing on wage increases in the form of higher prices to the customer was thought to be fuelling inflation. A Royal Commission under Lord Donovan investigated trade unions and employer associations (1968), and came to the conclusion that management should assume more direct responsibility for industrial relations, particularly by creating local grievance, discipline and dispute procedures and by creating a more professional approach to collective bargaining. The rise in the importance of industrial relations departments thus occurred, and a shift was seen towards more powerful management teams and an upgraded personnel function. Those experts in procedures and supervisors who had become enmeshed within the current industrial relations system were seen to be no match for well-trained shop stewards. Training of management within industrial relations was therefore given more priority as the move to local-level bargaining continued.

The expanding scale of employment and the increasing complexity of business operations had, by the 1920s, already led to a more bureaucratic management hierarchy, supported by a network of rules. The employment management tradition with its emphasis on control through systems was another source of identity for human resource specialists.[7] In 1926, when ICI was formed from the amalgamation of a number of small companies, a specialist was appointed to oversee the creation of a single set of working conditions and a common approach to personnel management. Lloyd Roberts was arguably the first specialist personnel manager, and in other large companies of the time an awareness was dawning that as management operations increase in scale so the need for a specialist in the personnel field becomes more pressing. By the 1930s there were management development policies being set up in corporations such as Pilkington's and Courtauld's, and the requirement for formal rules to deal with questions of promotion and salary/pay increases was understood by the larger companies.[6]

The important issue which still remains a concern for human resource specialists is how to retain control, especially among line managers, without having any line authority. Reporting systems, such as head count, budgets and statistical reports to answer questions on absenteeism, accidents, timekeeping and output, were a solution to this problem, not just for personnel specialists but also for 'time and motion' study experts, production control staff and the growing ranks of middle managers to whom they reported.

This bureaucratic tradition remains a source of negative opinion about personnel specialists, who are perceived as the guardians of the rules of work and experts in the minutiae of policies. Wage payment systems in particular gave rise to this aspect. The typical payment by results schemes which became more and more complex until the rules were beyond simple description, and were therefore open to endless disputes, are a good example. On the more positive side, personnel specialists imposed restrictions on the power of line managers to act unfairly and to abuse their power, and this has helped to create order and prevent organizational life from becoming anarchic.[7]

During both world wars these trends were given a further boost through government controls which personnel specialists frequently had to apply. For example, the dilution agreements with the trade unions had to be policed in the First World War, and in the Second World War the direction of labour rules had to be properly applied.

Currently, human resource specialists are heavily involved in 'downsizing' – that is, in managing redundancy schemes, with all the associated policies, such as outplacement and early retirement schemes. These operations require an efficient approach and accurate head counts and budgets.

Therefore the bureaucratic 'employment management' tradition is still very significant.

The associated tradition is that of 'professional' management. At the start of this century many managerial occupations began to set up separate professional associations as part of their move towards a specialist identity. Sales managers, accountants and the like were searching for techniques which would help them to contribute to the success of their companies. Personnel specialists have similarly been engaged in a quest for some scientific basis for their expertise.

This 'scientific origin' is still sought, but a partial answer has been found in the social sciences. Sociology, industrial psychology, occupational psychology, labour economics and statistics have helped to explain what is happening in organizations, and have provided techniques such as selection testing and techniques in fields such as employee development, manpower planning and communications.

The 'organization development' techniques, used to help organizations to change, are a mixture of individual-level work helping people to change and group work in teams. The industrial relations implications were often the difficult part of any change, but where these could be satisfactorily addressed (the application, for example, of semi-autonomous work groups with reduced management layers, better communications, improved supervision and appropriate rewards policies) were extremely effective from the 1970s onwards.[9]

Changes to the law have also given human resource experts another field in which to demonstrate specialized competence. Equal opportunity policies, discipline procedures, health and safety legislation and now industrial relations laws governing strike ballots and disputes have added to the procedural armoury possessed by human resource managers.

Perhaps the most important professional attribute now required is how to apply the skills, knowledge and techniques garnered from all four traditions in a particular organizational context. As discussed below, the movement towards a new approach to industrial relations and new demands on organizations combined with competitive pressures and the recession have heightened awareness of the human resource contribution to business success. This has come about in the UK because of recent fundamental changes to the prevailing political ideology, and because economic and social change are leading to the reappraisal and reform of many British institutions.

Developments in human resource management since 1979

The period since 1979 has marked a change in the field of employment and industrial relations. If we can summarize the 1970s as being a time when the industrial relations and employment management traditions came to the fore with changes to the law, the expansion of public sector trade unionism and an emphasis on systems and techniques, then the period from 1979 has seen a move on to human resource issues.[10, 11]

The Thatcher government was elected in 1979 on a mandate to change Britain's economic position and to reduce trade union power. The major purpose was to operate on a basis of 'sound money', that is, inflation was seen as the number-one enemy and trade unions as helping to create inflation by excessive wage claims and restrictive practices; excessive bureaucracy both in management and in government with too much interference in the working of the market were also given as further reasons for Britain's economic decline. The monetarist policies which were pursued with vigour helped to introduce this ideology to the populace as a whole. The government was quite clear about its objective in reducing trade union power and indeed this was a part of the Conservative Party manifesto. The attack on trade union power and the desire to reduce government expenditure as part of the broad economic strategy came together in the public sector management arena, so that public sector trade unions and local and central government civil servants felt under attack.[12] The Conservative government began the process of privatization and reducing the number of civil servants: a process which has continued through to the present day. The Thatcher government succeeded in reducing the number of central government civil servants by 250 000 and privatized many of the older industries which had been taken into public ownership at the end of the Second World War and subsequently. There was an increasing emphasis at this time on the City of London, and on service industries at the expense of manufacturing.

The method for reducing trade union power was first, to introduce changes to the law which removed from trade unions the immunities they had long enjoyed from actions for damages as a consequence of any strikes or industrial unrest with which their officials were associated. Consequently, sympathetic strikes and so-called secondary action were outlawed. In a move which was aimed at the rank and file, 'to return unions to their members', strict balloting procedures were to be adopted for the election of officials and balloting was also needed if industrial action was to be threatened. As a result of these changes trade unions found that any failure to follow the letter of the law resulted in employers taking civil actions against them in the courts which led to fines and the sequestration of trade union funds. There is no doubt that trade union militancy as measured by the number of days lost through strikes has been reduced since 1979. There have been set-piece battles, such as the miners' strike in 1984/5 which distort the general trend, but working people have been less inclined to challenge managerial prerogatives. The disputes which have occurred in the public sector have often been initiated because of a tacit public sector incomes

Table 2.1 *UK industrial disputes*

Year	No. of days lost (thousands)	No. of stoppages
1980	11 964	1 348
1981	4 266	1 344
1982	5 313	1 538
1983	3 754	1 364
1984	27 135[a]	1 221
1985	6 402	903
1986	1 920	1 074
1987	3 546	1 016
1988	3 702	781
1989	4 128	701
1990	1 903	630
1991	761	369
1992	524	358

[a] Year of the miners' strike.
Source: *Employment Gazette*.

policy. Various groups, including teachers, ambulance staff and civil servants, have found the government unwilling to endorse review body recommendations, and the automatic right to comparability between public and private sector employers is no longer accepted by the government.

The desire to reorganize the public sector along the same lines as in the private sector makes for a climate where the old public sector values are being challenged. The volume of new legislation, new structures (including agencies to carry out policies) and the piecemeal changes to the public sector have prevented a large-scale, head-on clash between public sector workers and the government. Instead we have seen a running battle of skirmishes over particular issues. The figures in Table 2.1 which show the decline in expressed militancy should therefore be interpreted in the light of high unemployment.

It could be argued that the trade unions were already suffering as a consequence of labour market changes. The increasing number of women in the workforce who typically were not trade union members and did not wish to join, the increasing number of part-time employees and the move away from the older 'smokestack' industries towards more modern businesses meant that the trade unions' normal recruiting grounds were disappearing. The white-collar trade unions were also not necessarily as militant as blue-collar unions and the members of these unions did not always support the Labour Party and its aims.

The recession of the early 1980s was mostly within the older industries. Unemployment was high in Scotland, Northern Ireland, the North of England,

Wales and in any of those areas which had been dependent on manufacturing, engineering, shipbuilding and mining. The south-east of England
was less affected and there was an impression that this recession was caused
by the inefficiencies of British industry and its failure to adapt to modern
needs. At the same time as the government was changing the law on industrial relations, employers were also on the offensive to change the nature of
industrial relations in the workplace. The 'new' industrial relations which
was emerging was a continuation of the trend towards company-level bargaining but with a difference. Companies now actively sought to reduce the
number of trade unions with whom they bargained, and to simplify their
bargaining arrangements. This was perhaps encouraged through the introduction of Japanese management practices in certain companies, such as
single-union agreements. Even in the older industries, flexibility and new
working practices were introduced. In particular, these were the removal of
demarcations between craft and semi-skilled workers, the increasing use of
flexible hours of work including annualized hours agreements as well as
flexitime and a more flexible use of employment contracts.[13] These flexible
contracts included casual, part-time and temporary staff who were used
more and more. By the end of the 1980s the position had been reached
where there were more people on non-standard contracts than there were
on standard ones. By that time there were approximately 5 million part-
time employees and 5 million self-employed people. In addition, there were
people who had created portfolio jobs which included working for a number
of employers. Increasingly, people worked at weekends or on shift arrangements which gave them time for their family or to work for someone else
during the week. There was also the introduction increasingly of franchise
arrangements. Outsourcing also began to become common. In these cases
companies sought cheaper workforces abroad to manufacture products
which were then marketed in the UK.

Many of these changes, which were perhaps brought about by the recession but which were encouraged by the government and by the felt need to
compete abroad against more efficient companies, meant that British industrial relations and human resource management were changing.[14] Not only
was human resource management changing but the very introduction
of the new human resource management policies was helping to change
organizations and to make them more efficient. It could be argued therefore
that in the case of the 1980s recession, human resource management helped
companies to become more competitive.

The new human resource management philosophies were based on individualism, especially in terms of rewards and personal contracts, and were
also characterized by a move to line management of the responsibilities for
such areas as discipline, grievance and disputes handling. Human resource
management became a source of expertise but not of executive action in

relation to the management of people. At this time companies were looking to produce flatter structures with fewer levels in the hierarchy and to shorten lines of communication. The industrial relations policies of the 1970s through which shop stewards had gained so much power were changing. Line managers were now seeking to communicate directly with the workforce and to create company cultures which were consistent with the company's mission and values. There was in this sense more employee involvement, although in not every company were quality circles and similar techniques adopted satisfactorily.

Changes from Europe emanating from the European Commission were seen to threaten this new approach to management. The Commission was thought to represent a return to a bureaucratic intervening style of government in which all the rules regarding work were laid down centrally with little chance for local autonomy and flexibility. The labour market changes in the UK were presented by the government as a 'freeing-up' of the labour market because, as a consequence of these changes, employers and employees had more choice about the way in which they worked and were able to make their own career decisions. At a time of full employment this may indeed have been the case. Changes from Brussels were therefore perceived as unnecessary and failing to meet the subsidiarity requirements which the government believed underpinned the European Community's work. The Thatcher government believed it had decentralized and moved decisions back down to organization levels in employment matters. The collectivist views from the Commission were therefore anathema to the British government in the late 1980s. In fact, many of the changes such as those relating to equal opportunities had already been passed into law in the UK and there already existed a network of individual employment rights which individuals had achieved during the 1970s and 1980s, many of which were common through Europe.

Current trends in human resource management

In the early 1990s a new recession occurred. There is evidence that this was a different kind of recession from the one which afflicted the UK in the 1980s. The permanently high levels of unemployment which seemed to have been reached (3 million plus in the UK) were found throughout Europe. The downturn in the economic cycle coincided with German reunification and consequential high levels of interest rates in Germany, the end of the cold war and therefore the end of arms manufacture, and a downturn in activity in the United States. The result of this recession was, therefore, that the whole of business found itself working at a reduced level, including the service sector. A feature of the 1989–93 recession is that service industries and the south-east of England were as badly hit as the older industries in the regions. In this recession, large companies found themselves vulnerable. The shedding of labour in companies which had long claimed to have a no-redundancy policy, such as IBM or Marks & Spencer, shows that however well intentioned those policies, the reality of economics forces policy changes beyond the power of management strategies to resist.

In this recession there seemed little the human resource function could do to assist in overcoming the effects on unemployment and the social hardship which was, and is now, experienced. One new emphasis which has occurred in the 1990s, however, is the importance attached to acquiring skills and qualifications. Management education has expanded substantially in the UK with over 120 different institutions offering MBA courses, for example, and the new emphasis on skills has been given a local presence through the creation of Training and Enterprise Councils. These 'TECs' are bodies which bring together employers, local authorities and other interested parties such as the educational providers to agree on training and development strategies for a particular area. The government has also been funding youth training schemes in an attempt to overcome some of the problems of youth unemployment, and there are a plethora of government and local initiatives to try to solve the immediate impacts of the recession. What seems to be lacking at present is an overall coordinated strategy to assist the training and development of people at all levels, and it is this particular approach which the Labour Party, having failed once again to be elected to office, is pressing on the government from the opposition benches.

The reduction of inflation to around 2–3 per cent has meant that the field of rewards itself is now changing. Whereas overall scale increases were common during the time of high inflation, more and more companies are now moving to performance-based pay. Increases in wages and salaries in such companies are therefore only awarded if the employees can show higher productivity or some improvement in performance.

Perhaps the most significant changes have been to organization structures. The process of flattening structures, that is, delayering and changing structures to be more responsive to the marketplace, has continued since the 1980s. Business process redesign, the reorganization of businesses around their customer requirements, using information technology strategically to deliver information when and where it is needed, and the move towards much smaller, more flexible structures has led some commentators to suggest that we are in a post-Fordist or post-Modernist stage of organization development, where organic approaches to structure are the norm and the large-scale mass production factories of the past are never likely to return. Post-Modernist in this context is intended to imply flexible, user- and customer-friendly, smaller organizations, which are expected to replace the large bureaucratic approaches of the 1960s and 1970s just as smaller more

individual buildings are replacing massive concrete structures in architecture. This is also a time when the large headquarters of companies have
been reduced and smaller corporate offices have sprung up which provide
only secretarial and other services for the top team, the remaining functions being devolved into divisions and/or companies at a local level. The
human resource function has, of course, been affected by these changes
as have all other specialist functions.

These changes to human resources are sometimes described as a move
from 'traditional personnel management' to 'human resource management'.[15]
The latter term is thought to describe a different approach to the management of people. The new approach develops employees as assets to the
business and seeks to improve their utilization and efficiency. Personnel
management under these terms is seen as an administrative function which
concentrates on what we have described as the employment management
tradition. Such a black-and-white picture is perhaps some way from the
truth. In reality, there were many different models of personnel management in operation in British industry since the Second World War, some of
which depended heavily on the professional tradition while others (for
example, in the nationalized industries) followed the industrial relations
tradition. However, the change that is seen in human resource management
is in the recognition of the strategic value of human resources. The human
resource management function is now represented on approximately half
the boards of British companies, and in all the major changes to corporations that have taken place, human resource directors have been seen
to play a major role. For example at British Airways, at BP or in the new
National Health Service organizations and in many other large-scale changes,
human resource direction has been seen to be essential. This is because
in most of these changes what has been required is a new philosophy of
management. Such a philosophy was often based on concepts of employee
commitment using the ideas of empowerment and restructuring to revitalize employees and to generate a more creative approach to their management. Management development strategies have been used heavily in this
process and such techniques as team building, action learning and personal
development activities have all been harnessed to the goal of inculcating a
new philosophy.

None of this would have been possible without a new approach to industrial relations. The changes which began in the 1980s therefore had long-
term significance. The reduction in trade union members by about 3 million
since 1979 is a reflection of the changes to occupation structures as well as
of the high levels of unemployment which the UK has suffered (see Table
2.2). There is also evidence, however, that the trade union agenda which
was based largely on early twentieth-century concerns has not been up-
dated to the needs of the late twentieth century. Trade unions have not

Table 2.2 *UK Trade unions with 100 000 members or more, membership in 1990*

Transport and General Workers Union	1 223 891
GMB	865 360
National and Local Government Officers Association	744 453
Amalgamated Engineering Union[a]	702 228
Manufacturing Science and Finance Union	653 000
National Union of Public Employees	578 992
Electrical Electronic Telecommunication and Plumbing Union[a]	366 650
Union of Shop Distribution and Allied Workers	361 789
Royal College of Nursing of the UK	288 924
National Union of Teachers	218 194
Union of Construction Allied Trades and Technicians	207 232
Confederation of Health Services Employees	203 311
Union of Communication Workers	202 500
Banking Insurance and Finance Union	171 101
Society of Graphical and Allied Trades 1982 (SOGAT)	168 753
National Association of School Masters and Union of Women Teachers	168 539
National Communications Union (Engineering and Clerical Groups)	154 783
Assistant Masters and Mistresses Association	138 571
National Graphical Association (1982)	129 575
Civil and Public Services Association	122 677
National Union of Mineworkers	116 252
National Union of Civil and Public Servants	113 488
National Union of Railwaymen	101 311
Total of trade unions with more than 100 000 members	8 001 574
Total for all unions	9 810 019

[a] These two unions are now merged to form the Amalgamated Engineering and Electrical Union.
Source: Annual Report of the Certification Officer 1991.

been able to mobilize women who now comprise 50 per cent of the working population to the same degree as they were able to mobilize men. They have found it difficult to penetrate the newer industries and to cope with the organization structure changes which have been occurring. The move towards smaller organizations and more flexible structures is again inimical to the bureaucratic trade union approach. Partly as a response to this and the felt need for more financial security we are seeing the emergence of new 'super-unions'. The first of these has been formed by the amalgamation of the two great unions of skilled employees, the engineers and the electricians and plumbers. This union, the Amalgamated Engineering and Electrical Trade Union, will therefore wield much greater power. Japanese investment in the UK has also had an impact on trade unions. Although still relatively small in numbers, Japanese companies have shown that it is possible to run car factories in a different way from the traditional approaches which were tried and which failed in the 1960s and 1970s. The single-status workforce, the total involvement of management with their employees, the use of quality circles, the high degree of discipline and training are all aimed at producing a quality product with the minimum waste and with the involvement of employees in the process. The management practices in these companies were not specifically Japanese but were just good management practice. We know that in Japan redundancies have been occurring as a consequence of the worldwide recession and there is no guarantee that, whatever the management practice that is adopted, the company will be successful.

We can summarize the changes which have currently taken place in British human resource management by saying that there is a new set of relationships now at work. The move to knowledge workers rather than manual workers, the changes in the nature of work itself with the introduction of new technology, the increasing number of casual, part-time and sub-contract workers, the large number of women now employed and the changes to organization structures have all helped to produce a new climate. Companies have, in varying degrees, capitalized on this new climate to become more efficient.

The major problems of unemployment which are faced by European societies are structural rather than problems which can be solved at the company level. New organization forms, including the highly automated factory and the use of information technology in business process redesign, lead us to believe that unemployment also has a technological base. The new philosophies of management which have been espoused by the leading-edge companies have been built on the assumption that empowerment, flatter structures and individualized approaches to management will produce high-quality products at a competitive price. The challenges for human resource management are in the societal rather than the company area. Increasingly, companies are taking on societal responsibilities for education and training, the disciplining of the workforce, health (non-smoking policies, screening, etc.), proper sexual behaviour (through the codes of practice to remove sexual harassment, for example) and the provision of benefits which previously might have been offered by the state.

The difficulties we are left with are that some actions are required at the societal level to promote employment and to create living and working conditions which are compatible with the ideals of Western democracy. The idea of the Social Charter which the British government rejected was to try to address these issues along with the changes to the common economic market, in order to show the people of Europe that there is more to the European Union than just improving the profits of the larger companies. Clearly, the interventionist, corporatist approach which was implied by the

Social Charter is no longer acceptable as a general approach to the management of society. What has yet to be proposed and the challenge to come is to find a way in which societal-level norms can be created without government itself taking on that responsibility.

The role of human resource managers has therefore been changing. This is now very much that of a change agent, consultant and adviser to line management. The representation of human resource management at board level is now often undertaken not by a specialist but by a senior line manager. This may mean that human resource management is at last seen as being too important to be left to some narrow specialist! This is perhaps as it should be, given that the need now is for societal integration by companies so that questions of employee development, standards of behaviour and ethical practice can be addressed.

References

1 Cole, G. D. H. and Postgate, R., *The Common People 1746–1946*, Methuen, London, 1961.
2 Thompson, E. P., *The Making of the English Working Class*, Pelican Books, London, 1968.
3 Mayhew, H., *London's Underworld* (ed. P. Quennell), Spring Books, London, 1950.
4 Child, J., 'Quaker employers and industrial relations', *Sociological Review*, November 1974.
5 Niven, M., *Personnel Management 1913–1963*, IPM, London, 1967.
6 Tyson, S. J., *Specialists in Ambiguity: the study of personnel management as an occupation*, PhD thesis, University of London, 1979.
7 Tyson, S. J. and Fell, A., *Evaluating the Personnel Function*, 2nd edn, Stanley Thornes, Cheltenham, 1992.
8 Hobsbawm, E. J., *Labouring Men. Studies in the History of Labour*, Weidenfeld and Nicolson, London, 1964.
9 Tyson, S. J. and Jackson, A., *The Essence of Organisational Behaviour*, Prentice Hall, Englewood Cliffs, NJ, 1992.
10 Storey, J., *New Perspectives on Human Resource Management*, Routledge, London, 1991.
11 Legge, K., 'Personnel management in recession and recovery', *Personnel Review*, **17**, November 1988.
12 Tyson, S. J., 'The dilemmas of civil service management', *Personnel Management*, September 1988.
13 Brewster, C. and Connock, S., *Industrial Relations: cost effective strategies*, Hutchinson, London, 1985.
14 Sisson, K. (ed.), *Personnel Management in Britain*, Basil Blackwell, Oxford, 1989.
15 Storey, J., *Developments in the Management of Human Resources*, Blackwell, Oxford, 1992.

3 Managing people in Germany
Karl Blum

Historical background: main features

On 3 October 1990, Germany regained its national unity. The previous territory of the Bundesrepublik Deutschland ('Federal Republic of Germany')
was extended by the five new *Bundesländer* ('regional states') Brandenburg,
Mecklenburg-Vorpommern, Sachsen, Sachsen-Anhalt and Thüringen. Furthermore, unified Berlin was declared the capital of the united Germany.
Thus the former territory of the Deutsche Demokratische Republik ('German Democratic Republic') became part of the European Communities with
the same rights and duties as other members.

   While establishing national unity the country is also faced with the task
of transforming East Germany's centrally planned economic system into the
kind of social market economy that has evolved in the Bundesrepublik
since the Second World War. For a social market economy and economic
development to be achieved, a basic framework and the legal foundations
need to be set up in East Germany. This includes, in particular, the concept
of private ownership, freedom of economic activity and of establishment,
open markets, free adjustment of prices and competition.

   The difficulties involved and the resistance to be overcome in this process
have so far been considerably underestimated. The idea that the market
mechanism alone would regulate a large part of the restructuring has proved
to be a misconception. Although employees are highly qualified, mass unemployment is spreading rapidly due to inadequate capitalization of East
German companies. Most of East Germany's capital stock proved – much
to everyone's surprise – to be useless. Almost all the companies were found
to be uncompetitive in world market terms. With traditional markets in
Eastern European countries being lost due to their economies collapsing
and their political systems breaking down, East German producers have
had considerable financial difficulties. Nor have their goods found ready
markets in the West either! To set up new enterprises and production
facilities takes time – a commodity in scarce supply. Furthermore, the qualifications of many employees need to be adapted. The most important

impediments appear to be widespread undercapitalization of companies and – very important in this context – inflexible property title regulations, both inherited from the Communist state. When returning state-owned property to private owners the principle of 'restitution before compensation' is applied. In many cases uncertainty about ownership is a result, entailing potential investors' inability to provide property as collateral for bank loans. This proves to be an important obstacle for the setting up of small and medium-sized enterprises. Furthermore, very large infrastructural problems require massive public funding. Consequently, the public debt in the Bundesrepublik Deutschland is soaring to a level unheard of since the Second World War. In addition, public funding is required for the multitude of measures relating to labour market politics.

The East German people are expressing their aspirations to reach the level of development and the standard of living of the people in the former Bundesrepublik as quickly as possible and are demanding a share in the social product that by far exceeds their productivity. This is another impediment to rapid growth in investment. Setting a viable economic policy for the new Bundesländer has therefore become a high-wire act. On the one hand, growing burdens and the lack of attractiveness of investment would considerably slow down economic development; on the other, increasing disappointment within the population would make a large-scale westward migration from the newly embraced territory a real threat. This is a consequence of the unified economic area.

After the Second World War a 'social market economy' was established in the Bundesrepublik against considerable opposition. This economic concept is based on the theories of the 'ordoliberal' school, in which the state has a primary role in fighting abuses of dominant market positions and excessive concentration by major companies and of safeguarding competition with appropriate measures. The prerequisites for such a form of market economy include a high degree of competition and free access to markets, i.e. the freedom of production, free trade including international trade, freedom of contract (as long as the rights of others are not curtailed), freedom of entrepreneurial decision under risk and private ownership of production facilities. With a view to regulating economic processes, this approach provides for a redistribution of the market income (GDP) by means of a progressive income tax as well as through socio-political measures for safeguarding the survival of the weaker economic entities and the protection of natural resources (see Exhibit 3.1).

The establishment of the social market economy after the Second World War was aimed particularly at freeing West Germany's productive forces by underlining the government's commitment to the principles of freedom of investment, freedom of consumption and freedom of competition. It was

Exhibit 3.1 *Ordoliberalism*[1]

'This term stands for the core message of the so-called "Freiburg School". Its objective is the deliberate formation of an open and constitutional society and its appropriate liberal market economy bound by social rules, namely in the field of competition. According to ordoliberalism, it is up to the democratically legitimated government (1) to bring about perfect competition in the interests of efficient use of the entire productive organization, of fair distribution of income and of the simultaneous pursuit of economic and social policies that are required and (2) to obviate concentrations of power that are uncontrolled by competition.

The ordoliberal programme is composed of principles that constitute economic order, i.e. framework (complete competition, free market access, monetary stability, consistency of economic policy, private property with full responsibility, freedom of contract) to regulate structural and process policies and to adjust the market mechanism and competition in the case of disturbances (monopolies, macroeconomic losses, social tensions). Market conformity is the decisive criterion in the choice of interventionist measures i.e. all interventions by government in the workings of the economy must influence it in the direction of an ideal market economy.'

strongly promoted by Ludwig Erhard (1897–1966), the first minister for economic affairs, as a means of discipline in maintaining and increasing the productivity of the market system with a wide-ranging ethos of social responsibility. Against this background the German *Wirtschaftswunder* ('economic miracle') was to develop in the 1950s.

During the cold war the smaller part of Germany, the German Democratic Republic, was fully integrated into the Communist Eastern bloc, while the Bundesrepublik with its liberal economic and social system sought a Western orientation and opened up to the world. In this context it is important to note that peoples' minds became internationally-oriented and that more cooperative forms of co-existence were practised as a new mode of behaviour. Thus European integration became a reality in the 1950s, with Germany and its citizens also participating in the global forms of international cooperation and the solution of problems on a worldwide scale. This represented a total break with the concepts of nationalism and autarky (economic self-sufficiency), dominant in Germany until the end of the Second World War (see Exhibit 3.2).

German unification therefore connotes a great challenge, because the people in the former GDR have to adapt their view of the world to the open perspectives of the West Germans. Such difficulties become visible, for example, in their relations with foreigners with whom the former GDR citizens were not supposed to consort.

Exhibit 3.2 *Friedrich List (1789–1848) and Germany's internal market*

In the preface to the first edition of his *National System* (1841) Friedrich List wrote: 'In those days the amazing effects of the Continental System and the destructive consequences of its abolition were still too obvious to be ignored. . . . It occurred to me that Germany would need to abolish its provincial customs areas and, through a common external tariff system, try to achieve the level of development other nations had already attained owing to trade policy.'

These words contain, in embryo, the whole system of List's economic theory: a nation's 'productive forces' that its customs policy may equally awake or destroy; the theory of stages of economic development, the highest being full 'industrial and commercial development' as observed in England, for instance; the concept of 'educational tariffs', by way of which, following Napoleon's example of the Continental System, the economy of the German nation was to be encouraged and urged on until competitiveness with the English industrial state was achieved.

List's 'national system' of economics and his fight against the free trade ideology, tailor-made for English conditions, were based not on theoretical reasoning but on practical experience and observation of the Continental System's positive effects on industrialization, made during the years from 1806 to 1816.

The German Empire's Customs Union remains his imperishable historical achievement; its preparation was his doing, and, during the crisis of the customs union concept (1843–1845), he, through his writings and his function as publisher of the customs union paper, was a major contributor to its preservation and strengthening.

Present political and economic system: main features

Germany's present political and economic system is currently subject to great strains. This is a natural consequence of the upheaval caused by unification. Other breaking-points are beginning to show as well. There are various indicators for this. It appears that the responsible politicians have to date failed to properly explain the process of European integration to the people; neither the burdens involved nor the advantages they are to enjoy, particularly the long-term development perspectives of Europe and its economic and social systems, seem to be fully appreciated by the population. Lack of acceptance and the danger of false or falsified information being used by certain elements to stir up emotions to disguise the underlying facts are serious consequences of such carelessness, as can be seen in the handling of questions of political asylum or in economic matters. Increasing involvement of Germany in international organizations and tasks on a worldwide scale are being discussed, as well as its future stance towards instruments of international conflict management. For much too long the Germans have used 'lack of sovereignty after the Second World War' as an excuse for negligible cooperation in major international issues. Quite understandably, fears regarding increased involvement are now being expressed in the population. More educational work needs to be done in this respect.

When the *Grundgesetz* (Basic Law) came into effect on 24 May 1949 the Bundesrepublik Deutschland was founded. This democratic, social and federal state includes the *Bundesländer* of Baden-Württemberg, Bavaria, Hesse, Lower Saxony, Northrhine-Westfalia, Rhineland-Palatinate, Saarland, Schleswig-Holstein, Bremen and Hamburg as well as West Berlin before the unification of both German states. As mentioned earlier, after unification on 3 October 1990 five new Länder were added, and Berlin became the capital of the unified Germany. Parliamentary democracy is Germany's form of government. The rule of law is one of its most important foundations, i.e. legality is the first principle of government action and is not to be put into question by a change of political leadership. State intervention in freedom and the right of private ownership requires formal legislation. Moreover, comprehensive protection by law is guaranteed. Although the principle of division of powers has been breached in some aspects, comprehensive control of government action is ensured through the federal system and mass media. The principle of social justice and the welfare state requires the government to balance social disparities. The main features of the free and democratic constitutional system are a multi-party system and the right of opposition. A restriction clause of 5 per cent in the electoral system prevents splinter parties from being established. The introduction of a 'constructive vote of no confidence' was to forestall a government from being overthrown by minorities. Free development of personality is guaranteed in the constitutional basic rights, such as the right to life, the right of physical integrity and the right of personal freedom. At the same time, opponents of the free and democratic constitutional system may not quote freedom in their support. Abuse of basic rights in the fight against the free and democratic constitutional system may result in these rights being forfeited. The German constitutional court is to review political associations and decisions with respect to their constitutionality.

Allegiance to the *Bund* ('federal government') is the main characteristic of the relationship between the federal government and the *Länder*. A *Land* failing to fulfil its constitutional or legal obligations may be obliged to fulfil them by the federal government with the consent of the federal council. Sovereignty for cultural affairs lies with the *Länder*, i.e. the federal government is responsible for setting only the legal framework; solely the extension and development of establishments of higher education is a joint task. In other cultural affairs, the *Länder* are responsible. Much federal legislation is carried out by the *Länder* as state authorities, i.e. only the legality of the execution is reviewed by the federal government; but the *Länder* also carry out federal legislation on behalf of the *Bund*. Within the limits of federal administration, the *Bund* sets up administrative bodies, such as the diplomatic service. Inter-level fiscal adjustment between the *Bund* and the *Länder* is due to fiscal legislation usually containing federal legislation, so that tax revenues need to be vertically distributed.

The President of the Federal Republic is head of state; the federal government is the executive branch and consists of the federal chancellor and the federal ministers. The chancellor (*Kanzler*) is elected by the *Bundestag* (federal parliament) at the proposal of the President and has the authority to establish the political guidelines within which the ministers manage their portfolios independently. In cases of differences of opinion between ministers the cabinet is to decide.

Although the Bundesrepublik's economic system is known as a social market economy, no rule to that effect is to be found in the *Grundgesetz*. However, a variety of liberal and social provisions incompatible with a centrally planned economic system are included in this constitutional framework law: guarantee of private ownership, right of inheritance, prohibition of expropriation without compensation, freedom to choose a profession and a job, prohibition of forced labour, freedom of movement, the right to establish economic associations, the principle of social justice and the welfare state, the social obligation of private property, etc. The *Grundgesetz* also obliges the *Bund* and the *Länder* to preserve general economic equilibrium (See Exhibit 3.3).

The principle of social justice and the welfare state is realized through guaranteed freedom of coalition, freedom to choose a profession, the capability of using private property in the public interest and the possibility of nationalization of land, natural resources and production facilities. Conflicts of social interest in the industrial sphere are mainly handled by the *Deutscher Gewerkschaftsbund* (Trade Union Federation), established in 1949, and the *Bund der deutschen Arbeitgeberverbände* (Employers' Federation), 1950.

The Stability Act 1967 requires the *Bund* and the *Länder* to consider the requirements of general economic equilibrium when taking economic and fiscal action. Measures taken are to contribute to the achievement of the economic goals of full employment, monetary stability, external equilibrium and continued and adequate growth (together with equitable distribution of income and wealth). The Act also forms the legal basis of trade-cycle orientated fiscal policy and concerted action, which is currently suspended.

In the brief history of the Bundesrepublik Deutschland a variety of instruments of conflict management for the labour market and systems of social provision have been developed. During the first years the law

Exhibit 3.3 *Social insurance in Germany*

The origin of social Insurance in Germany goes back to Chancellor Otto von Bismarck (1815–1898). His efforts to strengthen the Prussian-conservative character of the German Reich involve, besides the promotion of heavy industry and agriculture by customs protection, the pursuit of a range of social policies in order to divert workers from involvement with social democracy ideology.

After two attempts upon the Kaiser's life he pushed through the Reichstag (chamber of deputies) the so-called *Sozialistengesetze* in 1878. By means of this *anti-socialist legislation* the Social Democratic Party was submitted to stronger police control. Furthermore, meetings, groupings and publications were prohibited – also of unions – until 1890.

At the same time Bismarck introduced *social security legislation* with the obvious intention of inducing in workers a positive attitude towards the state. The worst consequences of labour conditions in those days were to be mitigated and the livelihoods of workers' families protected. With the so-called initial bills

- Health Insurance for Workers (1883)
- Accident Insurance (1884)
- Old-age and Invalidity Insurance (1889)

compulsory insurance was established by the Reichstag for low-wage workers. No doubt the German Social Democratic Movement could not be weakened decisively, but these legal provisions had a system-stabilizing effect and they prevented social turbulences.

During the first half of the twentieth century the social insurance system was continuously upgraded with regard to the insured as well as to increases of benefits and expansions of covered risks. The deeply-held idea of the social network established today among German employees dates back to these significant initiatives.

---

governing collective bargaining, protection against dismissal and the procedural rules for industrial dispute settlement were decided upon. The Co-determination Act, the Industrial Constitution Act and the Federal Personnel Representation Act followed. The Homework Act, the Maternity Protection Act and the Severely Disabled Persons Act are other important aspects of social policy. The Equalization of Burdens Act was aimed at equalizing war-induced burdens. Pension reform (dynamic pensions based on gross wages and salaries since 1957), the reform of statutory accident insurance and continued payment of wages are other landmarks of social policy. The Federal Public Assistance Act deals with state help for the individual claimant and the Employment Promotion Act has led to the establishment of a wide variety of measures of advanced vocational training and job creation. To this can be added the regional and sectoral structural measures carried out by the *Länder* in this field as well as the assisted areas support schemes, (e.g. zonal border development area). Wealth-formation schemes and savings promotion are aimed at achieving a more balanced distribution of wealth: premiums on building society savings, tax allowances, premium-carrying property-accumulation schemes for employees and tax privileges for saving through insurance are examples.

Key features in the current state of industry and commerce and their major effects

The Federal Republic of Germany is one of the world's major industrialized nations. Gross national product amounted to DM 1.85 trillion in 1985 (about DM 30 000 per capita), which put Germany in third place in an international ranking list, behind the United States and Japan. After unification, however, GNP per capita amounted to DM 40 530 in the West and DM 12 280 in Eastern Germany (1991).

International economic integration has been consistently pursued since the establishment of the Bundesrepublik, which founded the European Coal and Steel Community in 1951, together with France, Italy and the Benelux countries, and, in 1957, helped to create the European Economic Community and Euratom. Thus, European political union was to be achieved via economic integration.

The development of the Federal Republic's economic structure is similar to that of other industrialized economies. The number of people employed in agriculture has decreased considerably, as have the people employed in the productive sector. The service sector has increased but to a lower extent than in other developed economies such as the United States, the UK or France. Capital goods are the major industry in the productive and craft sector. Next in importance are the basic and manufacturing goods sector, consumer goods industry and food processing. These relative positions reflect a shift away from the food and consumer goods industries towards the capital goods industry after 1960. The latter is structured as follows (1991): vehicle construction (12.3 per cent), chemical industry (11.9 per cent), engineering (10.5 per cent), food industry (10.3 per cent), electrical engineering (10.1 per cent). Traditional industries, such as iron and steel (3.5 per cent), textiles (2.5 per cent), precision mechanics and optics (1.2 per cent) and office equipment (1.2 per cent) are of minor importance. Comparison of growth gives a different ranking (based on turnover 1980 = 100): office equipment (251), vehicle construction (145), chemical industry (141), electrical engineering (134) and engineering (128). As to regional distribution of

economic activity, other important industrial centres besides the traditional Ruhr Valley are agglomerations in Southern Germany (Stuttgart,
Munich, Nuremberg), the Rhine–Neckar area, Cologne–Düsseldorf,
Hannover and around the maritime ports of Hamburg and Bremen. This
regional differentiation turns out to be no serious impediment to economic
development, as the country's infrastructure is highly developed and
efficient.

The overall picture has changed because of unification of the two German
states. The production facilities and infrastructure of the former German
Democratic Republic proved to be in a desolate state at the time of transition. Therefore a very large transfer of capital towards East Germany was,
and is still, required. Such transfers amounted to about DM 140 billion
in 1991, more than 50 per cent of the 1989 GNP of the former GDR. DM
81 billion were provided by the federal budget, DM 35 billion by the
Fonds Deutsche Einheit ('German Unity Fund') and DM 12 billion by the
Gemeinschaftswerk Aufschwung Ostdeutsch-land ('joint operation recovery East
Germany'). A considerable part of the funds is allocated to stimulation of
investment activity and measures to improve the infrastructure. Private
investment is mainly directed towards production, especially the metal and
electrical engineering industries. Investment activity centres around the
Erfurt–Dresden axis. It is the job of the *Treuhandanstalt* (THA, 'Trust Fund'),
a federal agency, to privatize the production facilities nationalized under
the GDR regime. To date (1992), about 6000 out of 10 000 companies have
been transferred to new owners. Engineering and vehicle construction are
the most important industries in the new *Länder*, with regard to both their
share in total output as well as the number of companies (1990: 1800) and
people employed (1989: 962 000; 1990: 582 000). Further redundancies are to
be expected. About 80 per cent of the companies in these industries are still
under THA administration. With 50 per cent of output going to Eastern
European countries these industries' dependence on intra-bloc trade exceeded
that of any other industry. An estimated 300 000 jobs were directly dependent on these exports. With a market economy in place and Eastern markets
collapsing, the structural weaknesses of these industries quickly became
obvious, especially in vehicle construction. As demand forecasts for cars in
East Germany and the Eastern European countries were good, West German car manufacturers were quick to move in and to build new production
facilities. Engineering (machine tools, printing presses, textile machines, food-
processing machines, packing machines) is expected to become competitive
fairly quickly. The same is true for power machines, internal combustion
engines, tracked-vehicle manufacturing, clutches and gearboxes, hydrau-
lic equipment and environmental technology. Shipbuilding and chemical
equipment, in contrast, are expected to decline. Electrical engineering, electronics and appliances, precision mechanics and optics, communications

technology, microelectronics, office information technology and measuring and control engineering are also adjusting production to Western quality levels while considerably reducing their workforce. This, of course, requires heavy investment. The federal postal administration Telekom, for example, announced plans to invest some DM 55 billion until 1997. Other likely candidates for successful structural change include consumer goods and the food-processing industry.

The Federal Republic's economy has a strong international orientation. Some 25–30 per cent of GNP are exported. The EU is the main trading partner, absorbing more than 50 per cent of exports, while another 20 per cent goes to the ex-EFTA countries. Trade relationships with other Western industrialized countries are also important. About 5 per cent of foreign trade is with the OPEC countries. At present no current figures on trade with East European countries are available due to the collapse of these markets. Moreover, East Germany's influence on foreign trade is very difficult to estimate. Industrial products (vehicles, machines, chemical and electrical engineering products) account for about 90 per cent of all exports (by value), while imports of industrial goods have also risen considerably during the past few years.

The legislative framework for managing people and major features of the systems

Education

The Federal Republic's educational system is highly structured. Schooling is compulsory for children aged six to eighteen; during these years a minimum of nine years of full-time school is required. Schools providing general, vocational and higher education may be distinguished. The primary sector consists of four years of primary school and is followed by the secondary sector, comprising stage one, which includes two types of secondary modern school and grammar school up to the tenth form, and stage two, grammar school up to the *Abitur* (general university entrance qualification) at the end of the thirteenth form (UK GCE A-levels equivalent). Twelve years of full-time school are a minimum requirement for admission to German Fachhochschulen. An orientation phase during the fifth and sixth forms helps to guide the pupils as to which type of secondary school they should attend: either the first type of secondary school (Hauptschule, five or six years) or the second type (Realschule, six years) or grammar school (nine years). Some *Länder* have introduced comprehensive schools, comprising all three types of secondary schools. In the tertiary sector, university admission is via the *Abitur*. Admission to Fachhochschulen requires twelve years of full-time school and some time of practical training. While universities provide traditional scientific education, the Fachhochschulen are more geared towards the practical application of scientific contents. There are tendencies towards a higher degree of permeability between the different types of institutions of general and higher education.

Direct transition from secondary education to the vocational training system, comprising all officially recognized professions in industry, commerce and the crafts, is possible. This system usually caters for young people and provides their first professional training. This dual system is based either on an apprenticeship contract with a particular company or on vocational training institutions on an above-company level, and is supervised by the chambers of handicrafts and commerce. Practical training is complemented by theoretical education in vocational and technical schools and usually lasts about three years. Theoretical education is part-time, usually on one to two days a week, for a total of eight to twelve lessons a week.

The quaternary sector of the educational system comprises adult training, in the forms of general or qualifying further education. It is of increasing significance.

Although it should be in the companies' own best interest to provide traineeships to attract and bind qualified junior staff, political initiatives to secure the provision of sufficient numbers of training places appear to be necessary. Junior management is largely recruited from universities. The Fachhochschulen have had considerable success in this field since 1970, as their engineering and business management graduates in particular, are in high demand, and to their practically and – in an increasing number of cases – EU-oriented training.

Trade unions

The *Deutscher Gewerkschaftsbund* (trade union confederation) is the umbrella organization of 17 trade unions (organized by industry) of workers, employees and civil servants, representing almost 10 million members. Other organizations include the *Deutsche Angestelltengewerkschaft* (employees' union) and civil servants' unions (see Exhibit 3.4).

The trade unions' mission is to represent labour's economic, social and cultural interests. Their main interest lies in wage policy, but they are also specifically pursuing moves towards the humanization of work, reduction of working hours and social management of problems caused by mechanization and rationalization. Thus, for example, the 38-hour working week, a goal long fought for by the trade unions, has recently been achieved. The strike is the unions' most drastic – but most unwillingly employed – tool in

Exhibit 3.4 *European workers' representation at Volkswagen*[3]

> 'European employee meetings are *en vogue*. The number of companies involved in such activities is approaching 50. It is to be expected that over the next two years many companies of a European dimension anxious to create a cooperative labour climate will establish their own model. The pioneers' practical experiences have been positive and are encouraging other companies to become involved as well. Such activities are to be discussed here, for after years of fruitless declarations from the conference table it is now up to the practitioner to raise his voice.
>
> The European Volkswagen Group Works Council (EuroGWC) was established by the employee representations of the most important European VW manufacturing companies. Represented are the works in Wolfsburg, Hannover, Braunschweig, Kassel, Emden and Salzgitter (all VW AG), Ingolstadt and Neckarsulm (both Audi AG), Barcelona, Martorell and Pamplona (all SEAT SA) as well as Volkswagen Bruxelles.
>
> Employee representatives of Skoda and Volkswagen Bratislava are already participating in the meetings as well. The EuroGWC therefore represents the interests of over 90 per cent of all employees of the group's European automotive activities.'

industrial action. Therefore, the procedures to be adhered to during labour disputes are regulated in detail. The legal basis for industrial action, including strike and lock-out, follows from the freedom of coalition, as laid down in the Basic Law. Jurisdiction has made it clear that, in a legitimate strike, neither the trade unions nor the employers, when they lock out, act unlawfully. While public employees are permitted to go on strike as well, civil servants are not. Strikes need to be measures of collective industrial action. According to the Industrial Constitution Act, labour disputes within a shop or within the public service are prohibited for both sides of industry. Industrial action which violates the collectively agreed obligation to keep the peace is illegal and may result in damages being awarded. Generally, industrial action is considered a last resort, to be used only after all other possibilities have failed. Picket lines, for example, must not, by force or using threats, impede those willing to work from doing their job. After a wage agreement has expired – and with it the obligation to keep the peace – collective negotiations may break down. Most union statutes stipulate that strike ballots be taken only after the breakdown of pay talks has been officially declared. Wild-cat and protest strikes are possible in support of these ballots. The strike itself may be temporary or not limited in time. It may cover all or only a part of the organization's striking employees. The strikers may remain absent from their workplace or carry out a sit-down strike or go slow. At all times, measures taken need to be commensurate with the aims to be achieved, and the economic ruin of the opponent must not be caused. Moreover, the thrust of the strike must relate only to the content of the wage agreement. As contracts of employment are suspended during a strike, the strikers are not entitled to either wages and salaries or to unemployment benefits.

Rather, union members are paid strike benefits from union strike funds. Once a new wage agreement has been settled, the obligation to keep the peace begins anew. All strikes going beyond this legal framework are breaches of contract and authorize the employer to give notice of termination to the participants. Demonstration strikes in resistance against attacks on the constitutional order are the only exception to this rule, backed by the Basic Law.

Co-determination

One of the central principles of the social market economy is *Mitbestimmung* ('co-determination'). Co-determination is aimed at bringing democracy to companies and at controlling economic power by giving labour and capital a more equal status. Implementation has taken place on different levels:

1 Co-determination above company level means employee participation in the administration of the economy and in economic legislation. Thus, employees are represented in the self-governing institutions of the health and pension insurance funds. Union collaboration in the concerted action, envisaged in the Stability Act, may also be interpreted as an element of above company level co-determination.
2 Co-determination on a company level implies employee participation in the general management of the company through elected worker representatives in the governing bodies. In case of parity co-determination equal representation of employees and shareholders on the company's supervisory board is required. This type of co-determination is only applicable in companies with a 1000+ workforce in the coal, iron and steel industries, whose predominant activities are in the coal- or iron ore-extracting or iron- and steel-producing fields. An equal number of employee and shareholder representatives plus one non-committed member constitute the supervisory board, consisting of a total of eleven, fifteen or twenty-one members, depending on company size. The neutral member is appointed by proposals from both sides. An employee representative is also to be appointed to the board of management. The right of nomination for the employee representatives on the supervisory board lies with the trade unions. Since 1988 parity co-determination has also been applicable at group level, provided the group employs more than 2000

people and its turnover in the coal, iron and steel industries is in excess of 20 per cent of its total turnover (see Exhibit 3.5).

Exhibit 3.5 *Employee involvement*

'Following the publication of the MIT study by Womack, Jones and Roos (1991) and the rapid spread of the "lean-production" concept in German and West European industry, an idea is being revived that, after faint-hearted attempts in the 80s, threatened to sink into oblivion: employee participation in decision making and problem solving within the company.

Conventional company strategy is mostly aimed at minimizing decision risk and the related investment outlays, for instance when introducing new technologies, at all cost, i.e. usually with the help of expensive external consultants. The alternative is an in-house approach. Employees as internal experts may use their experience and knowledge for the benefit of the company and contribute to a more efficient decision making process.

The differences are obvious: Paying the bill usually means the end of the traditional approach which reliably leads to proposals – if occasionally of doubtful value – on how to solve the problem. If enforced, such standard concepts, whose top-down approach often prevents the real problems on the shop-floor from being taken into consideration, fail to win employee acceptance and entail insufficient identification with the project's objectives and a mostly half-hearted realization of its contents. Potential outcomes of this approach therefore include a short duration of the project and the installation of costly white elephants.'

Another important piece of legislation is the Co-Determination Act of 1976, applicable for companies with a 2000+ workforce. Issues of prime importance for the company, such as capital increases, winding-up or change of the object of the company or mergers are excluded from co-determination. An equal number of employee and shareholder representatives are appointed to the supervisory board (*Aufsichtsrat*), the total growing with the size of the company. Employee representatives may be recruited from workers, employees and managerial staff, with respect to their share in the company's workforce. If the chairman and the vice-chairman of the supervisory board fail to get a two-thirds majority, the chairman is elected by the shareholders and the vice-chairman by the employee representatives. In case of equal voting the decision is made by the chairman. The task of the supervisory board is, of course, to supervise the board of management (*Vorstand*). A labour relations manager is to be appointed to the board of management as a full member.

Simple co-determination on the basis of the Industrial Constitution Act of 1952 is applicable to companies with less than 2000 employees. This

provides for a third of the supervisory board to consist of employee
representatives, elected by secret ballot by the employees. A minimum of
two of the representatives need to be employed by the company.

Public debate on co-determination at company level is still continuing,
especially the enlargement of simple co-determination. Discussion here
centres on provisions being included in wage agreements to the effect of
bringing the number of employee representatives on the supervisory board
to parity rule.

3 Co-determination at plant level is also based on the Industrial Constitution Act and signifies employee participation – in the form of a works
council – in decisions concerning personnel, social, economic and organizational issues. If requested by the employees, a works council must be
established in each company employing more than five people, its members being elected by secret ballot. Employers or management must grant
this works council a hearing prior to making decisions concerning changes
in working conditions and production methods as well as investments
and staff matters, including, for example, holiday scheduling, changes in
working hours or special arrangements, recruitments, redundancies and
transfers. Management retains the sole right of decision, however, but
will, as a rule, endeavour to maintain good relationships with the works
council and its chairman. The Industrial Constitution Act also requires
the works council's prior consent on some issues (for example, on social
matters). On principle, employers may not proceed in these matters without the works council's prior approval; an arbitration board or a labour
court may be appealed to on controversial issues. Individual employee
participation rights are also provided for in the Industrial Constitution
Act. These are rights of being notified or heard or of discussion in matters
having a direct impact on the individual employee or his or her job.
Complaints may either be directed to management or brought forward
through the works council.

The banks' influence

A study of the relationship between the German banking system and major
industrial companies is important for an understanding of the strategic
thrust of German commerce. Their purpose is to assure ownership as well
as to provide strategic support for long-term planning. The following
account provides a detailed overview of key relationships.

The number of participating shareholdings in leading German companies
of the five banks combined (see Table 3.1) shows a steady increase from
twenty (1972) to 33 (1990). The number of shareholdings of the three major
banks has risen from eighteen (1972) to twenty-eight (1990). Temporary
trade investments are not included in these figures. Recently it was disclosed

Table 3.1 *Participating interests in top 100 companies held by the five banks most involved in industrial shareholding, from 1972 to 1990*[5]

	1972	1975	1978	1980	1982	1984	1986	1988	1990
Deutsche Bank (1)	9	9	10	10	10	11	11	13	14
Dresdner Bank (2)	5	5	5	5	5	7	7	7	8
Commerzbank (3)	4	5	6	7	7	7	8	7	7
								Total major	
Three banks (1–3)	18	19	21	22	22	25	26	27	29
WestLBank and Bayerische Ver-einsbank (4)	2	2	4	4	3	4	4	4	5
Total 5 Banks	20	21	25	26	25	29	30	31	34

that Deutsche Bank, Dresdner Bank and Bayerische Vereinsbank each hold a 10 per cent stake in Allianz-Holding, Germany's largest insurance company, which ranks twenty-second in the list of the country's largest companies. Thus, the 1990/1991 figures need to be increased to thirty-six participating interests for all five banks combined and to thirty for the three major banks.

If the major banks' shareholdings are subdivided into three categories (5–10 per cent, 10–25 per cent and 25–50 per cent stake) it becomes obvious that Deutsche Bank has expanded its investments mainly in the 10–25 per cent category. Dresdner Bank has increased its interests in the same category, invested in the 5–10 per cent category for the first time and decreased its exposure in the 25–50 per cent range as has Commerzbank, which in its turn added equity investments in the 10–25 per cent category to its portfolio and expanded interests in the 5–10 per cent range. For all five banks together, there is a considerable increase in participating interests in the lower and middle and a moderate decrease in the upper category.

Both analytical approaches, the first regarding banks' industrial interests in the 100 largest industrial companies in 1986, as well as the second, examining statistics compiled by the monopoly commission ranging from 1972 to 1988 (including updates up to 1990), provide ample proof that banks' participating interests in the largest German companies have risen considerably from 1972 to 1990. It was the three major banks and – although well behind – two other named banks which acquired stakes in the top 100 German companies. Other banks either do not have appreciable shareholdings or have sold them off.

A relationship between the aggregate voting rights exercised by banks and the aggregate number of seats and presidencies they hold on supervisory boards of companies would thus appear to have been established. The case of establishing a direct relationship between the interest share or the quota of proxies, on the one hand, and representation on the supervisory board, on the other, for individual companies and individual banks is a more difficult issue, especially in the light of the representation of other groups (workforce, management, etc.) on such boards which oversee all corporate activities within individual concerns.

It is worth noting that in eight leading German companies, banks hold interests of more than 25 per cent of capital stock. The banks hold

- Two directorships
- The presidency
- The presidency and an additional directorship
- The presidency and two additional directorships

in two cases respectively. Furthermore, banks hold another eight interests of between 10 per cent and 25 per cent, holding the presidency in two and one directorship in five companies. Finally, eight interests of between 5 per cent and 10 per cent are matched by eight directorships, among them one presidency and one vice-presidency. There are two cases in which banks hold directorships despite interests of less than 5 per cent. Furthermore, there are five cases in which interests of between 5 per cent and 10 per cent are not matched by corresponding directorships. Four of these interests are held indirectly. The only majority stake to be found is matched by a presidency.

On the whole, twenty-four equity holdings in various interests held by banks correspond to thirty-two directorships – of which ten are presidencies – held by these banks. Two directorships in cases of stakes not exceeding 5 per cent are to be added. Obviously, in most cases a blocking minority entails the bank holding the presidency and/or several directorships. In each case an interest of 10 per cent or more entails representation on the supervisory board, whereas interests of between 5 per cent and 10 per cent are often – but not always, especially not if held indirectly – matched by a directorship.

The significance of this analysis relates to the elementary strengthening of the German company's position that is provided by the security of having a major bank as a key shareholder. Such support is central to the model of industrial corporatism. It can also be a major life-saving aid as the receivership cases of the major German companies Klöckner, Metallgeschäft and Schneider show. It should be noted that, while smaller private enterprises are run by a general manager, public limited companies and private limited companies with a 500+ workforce are always supervised by a supervisory board with up to twenty-one members, depending on company size. The supervisory board's task is to appoint the board of management, whose members need to be reappointed every five years. Management policy and important decisions are made by the executive directors, who may be responsible for their own portfolios or for a special function, but responsibility for the company's general management is borne collectively by the board of management. Its chairman or its spokesman acts as representative in dealings with third parties.

Directors also coordinate the functions of middle management. Usually a hierarchical structure is to be found below board of management level. Assignments, functions and their interrelationships are precisely defined. Procedures of cooperation are laid down in detail, e.g. adherence to official channels.

Salient features of management practice

The term 'human resources management' comprises all institutions and measures aimed at providing labour for the fulfilment of managerial or goal-oriented tasks, in the quantity and quality required, at the right time and place and for the right period. Staffing requirements need to be ascertained first, with a surplus over a specified payroll resulting in layoffs and a deficit resulting in recruitments. Possibilities of enhancing employee qualifications and adapting them to structural changes within the company through further training are also to be taken into consideration in this context (see Exhibit 3.6).

Exhibit 3.6 *Motivation for work* [6]

'A large number of surveys, the Eurobarometers, carried out in the 70s and 80s with financial support from the EC, show that moral concepts have changed fundamentally throughout the western hemisphere. The way the results correspond between countries is also fascinating. If "prosperity" mattered most then, "quality of life" is today's buzzword. Consequently, the nature and the quality of labour are changing. Routine activities are being taken over by computers; on the other hand, more job autonomy for the individual is being demanded.

The B.A.T. Leisure Research Institute survey of September 1992 shows demand for shorter hours has decreased since 1988, for instance. Keenness at work has become the most important job content factor, i.e. a job is expected to provide diversity, challenge and a sense of achievement. Almost one out of two employees will be motivated to improve performance only through "meaningful job content", which supports the above results. People always aspire to what they have not yet achieved or what they experience as a deficit for themselves. Current employee clamour for a job that is both "fun" and "meaningful" points towards a new, qualitatively different level of aspiration in the labour force, who is no longer content with "a little more spare time" here and "a little more vacation" there.'

Recruitment is concerned mainly with the procurement of labour on the basis of contracts under private law, in the form of either workers for predominantly physical and mechanical activities or employees for predominantly mental and intellectual activities. Careful study of the labour market is imperative for systematic recruiting. Current as well as future labour supply need to be assessed. There are basically two ways of filling a vacancy: to recruit from either internal or external sources. When a position becomes vacant, the works council may demand in-house recruitment; should the company fail to comply, the works council may refuse approval of any recruitment or transfer planned in this context. A transfer, i.e. assignment to a different working group or to another department, may be by instruction from the employer (with remuneration not to fall below that of the previous job) or by notice of termination pending a change of contract; the latter being used if the standards of the new position do not correspond with the conditions of the current contract of employment. In this case the employer gives notice *ex parte* and, at the same time, offers a new employment contract at usually less favourable conditions. The works council must be consulted prior to the transfer and may withhold its consent. Recruiting will be from external sources if internal recruiting appears not to be viable. In such a situation, recourse will be taken to the labour office, to job advertisements in newspapers or to personnel consultants. Temporary labour may be leased for short-term employment.

The administration of employment in the Federal Republic of Germany is the role of the federal employment office, which has the exclusive right of dealing with job vacancies and vocational counselling. Labour exchanges or job centres in every important regional centre are entrusted with the management of placement services. Special placement services are available for specialists and specially qualified skilled labour and managerial staff. The central bureau in Frankfurt-am-Main caters for university graduates and senior executive staff. Key factors for the success of job advertisements include the selected medium's target group as well as timing and design. Due to the placement monopoly of the employment office, personnel consultants are only allowed to counsel on recruiting, with counselling covering a potentially wide range of activities, such as drafting of job requirements, conducting interviews or counselling on the decision and the conditions of employment. Finally, temporary labour, for example, for clerical work reduces – at increased cost – the risk of misjudgements in recruitment. Conditions are laid down in the Temporary Labour Act of 1972.

Personnel management attempts to influence employee behaviour in a performance-oriented way. Among its various instruments, structural elements, especially wages and salaries, job design and the management of cooperation between individuals and groups, are to be found. Personnel management occurs between the executive and subordinates, with the objective of assignments being accomplished and the working group's existence being preserved. The principal is empowered to give instructions to his or her subordinates within the limits of their employment contracts and needs to take their interests into account. Employees may freely express their opinion as long as no legitimate company interests are violated. The employee is also free to decide on his or her outward appearance, provided no uniform is obligatory and no customer expectations are seriously affected. On principle, the employee may not be prevented either from smoking during working hours or from drinking alcoholic beverages during a break. Instructions concerning behaviour outside official functions may only be given to employees in higher positions, provided they are in furtherance of the company's interests. If management styles, techniques and instruments are synchronized, we speak of a management model. The 'Harzburg model' approach to management has become well known in Germany. Job descriptions and management instructions containing principles of operation are its main tools. However, with the number of organizational rules in excess of 3000, it has proved to be bureaucratic, static and insufficiently sensitive. Regular performance appraisals, long neglected in German companies, have been increasingly introduced in recent years.

Wage and salary policy is an important part of human resources management, involving complex issues such as wage levels and wage fairness. The legal framework is laid down in collective wage agreements, labour–management agreements and individual employment contracts. Wage agreements, in skeleton form, contain general provisions on wages and salaries as well as on time rates, payment by piece rates, classifications, allowances, wage guarantees in case of transfer and sick pay, and usually remain in force for several years. Salary agreements, on the other hand, are usually made on an annual basis. These define wage or salary brackets, wage or salary scales, local cost-of-living allowances or performance bonuses. Wage scales within brackets are expressed in percentage terms of a specified hourly rate within a specific wage bracket. Wage agreements may be concluded between trade unions and trade associations (collective agreement) or between companies and trade unions (company pay scale). Job rating evaluates job content and job requirements and relates them to standard performances, using analytic or non-analytic methods. On this basis, wage scales for different levels of employee requirements may be determined. Wages may then be computed, using adequate payment systems such as time rates, piece rates or time rates plus premium wages.

In addition to agreed wages, companies also provide other important social services to their staff. These may include direct services, such as travelling allowances or holiday pay, and staff posts, such as company doctors or library managers. As these social services can account for as much as 50 per cent of indirect personnel costs, special attention needs to be given to their design and administration.

Human resources development is another important element, as, from a socio-economic perspective, it is a major contributor to vocational training. To acquire their first professional training, craft and commercial apprentices pass through the dual educational system, being trained in-house as well as in vocational schools (see above). Thereafter, further education to enhance their skills and qualifications is of ever-increasing importance.

Among the various ways of termination of employment, notice of termination is of special significance. Employers need to consider the following unfair dismissal provisions. Workers may have their jobs terminated at a fortnight's notice to the end of a week, this period increasing up to 3 months to the end of a quarter for workers aged over 35 whose length of service exceeds 20 years. Employees must be given 6 weeks' notice to the end of the quarter, and up to 6 months to the end of the quarter provided the employee's seniority is in excess of 12 years, his or her age is over 30 and the company employs more than two people. Notices of resignation must be given at a fortnight's notice to the end of the week (workers) or at 6 weeks' notice to the end of the quarter (employees). Employers need to comply with a variety of restrictions on giving notice. A notice is invalid if it is socially unjustified (if, for instance, the employee could be given another job within the company); it is prohibited during pregnancy and within a 4-month period after confinement; it is prohibited for handicapped people without prior consent from their social services department; it is prohibited during military or community service; it is prohibited for works councillors and youth representatives; it is invalid if the works council has not been consulted since it may object to the notice. Continued employment until the end of the proceedings is guaranteed, should the case be brought to a labour court. Instant dismissal may only be given for an important reason, such as theft, repeated refusal to work, intrigue against colleagues or unauthorized leaving of the workplace. The works council also needs to be consulted in these cases.

Wholesale redundancies are defined as dismissals of more than 10 per cent of the workforce within a 4-week period or of more than 30 per cent in companies with a 500+ workforce. In these cases, the works council needs to be notified early, and the labour office must be informed in writing, with a comment by the works council to be included. A social compensation plan may be worked out between the employer and the works council, containing provisions on, for example, redundancy payments, assumption of costs for job search, overreaching clauses for company loans, maintenance of company pension schemes or continued use of company flats. Staff administration is concerned with the organizational handling of human resources management, such as personnel data administration (with data protection being a critical issue), payroll accounting, administration of social services or personnel statistics (see Exhibit 3.7).

Exhibit 3.7 *Job protection: the case of Rostock*[7]

'The shock of the opening-up of the economy immediately took effect on the labour market, the number of unemployed quickly rising to more than 40 000. The abrupt transition from a centrally planned economy to a free market economy put considerable strain on labour market policy. In the spring of 1992 less than 60 per cent of the people of employable age in the Rostock labour market district were in regular employment, almost 40 per cent were socially cushioned by various instruments of labour market policy.

Transformation of the economy and the labour market does not only require the setting free of market forces but also goal-oriented and harmonized economic and labour market policies. Job creation programmes are an important measure to prevent employees from sinking into chronic unemployment. Vocational training and rehabilitation have been widely accepted in the region. Harmonization of vocational training and rehabilitation with the medium- and long-term qualification requirements of industry and regional and local authorities needs to be improved but meets with difficulties due to the lack of signals from the labour market. Job-creation schemes are an important factor in the region's structural change. The economic perspectives for the Rostock region require, at least for the medium-term, increased implementation of specific active instruments of the secondary labour market.'

Finally, it should be pointed out, that in Germany – as in other countries – human resource management – like other managerial functions – is subject to considerable restructuring due to the rapid spreading of microelectronics, rationalization and the implementation of new technologies on a broad scale. Increasingly, these rationalizations lead to a reorganization of all operational procedures, in order to optimize individual processes as well as their combined effects. External procurement, processing and distribution processes are redesigned using recent concepts of industrial logistics. The implementation of flexible production systems, computer-aided design (CAD), computer-aided manufacturing (CAM) and their integration to computer-integrated manufacturing (CIM) will, in the foreseeable future, lead to a complete reorganization of companies and, together with integrated office information systems, bring about new organizational structures, making in-house training an ever more vital factor of success. At the same time, the abolition of intra-EU barriers to trade and mobility will lead to an increase of exchange and trigger off various other impulses, so that features typical of German companies will disappear over time and concepts of nationally oriented management will no longer be needed in Europe.

References

1 Boelcke, W. A., 'Liberalismus', *HdSW*, **V,** Stuttgart, 1980.
2 Schmoelders, G., *Geschichte der Volkswirtschaftslehre*, Wiesbaden, 1961, p. 45
3 Schuster, H., 'Schon kein Experiment mehr: Der Europäische Volkswagen-Konzernbetriebsrat', *Personaliführung*, Düsseldorf, January 1993, p. 40.
4 Lindinger, C. and Ruhnau, J., Mitarbeiterbeteiligung, notwendige Vorgehensweise bei Umstrukturierungsprozessen, Strategie Umsetzung, Probleme', *Personaliführung*, Düsseldorf, February 1993, p. 116.
5 Bohm, J., *Der Einfluss der Banken auf Grossunternehmen*, Hamburg, 1992, p. 45.
6 Opaschowski, H., 'Auf dem Weg zur Arbeitswelt 2000, von der Pflichterfüllung zur Lebensfüllung, Folgen und Folgerungen', *Personalführung*, Düsseldorf, March 1993, p. 232.
7 Heseler, H. and Warich, B., 'Strukturwandel, Beschäftigung und Arbeitsmarktpolitik in Rostock', *Mitteilungen aus der Arbeitsmarkt- und Berufsforschung*, Stuttgart, March 1992, p. 289.

4 Managing people in France
Philippe Trouvé

Religious and family influences on French industrialization

France is a country with Catholic traditions. This, according to the sociologist Max Weber,[1] should be sufficient to categorize it. Unlike traditionally, commercially-minded Protestant countries, the French have always been noted for their deep mistrust of the business world and of the profit motive. This Catholic ideology would explain, according to some, France's late industrialization. Indeed, parts of France – most notably the south[2] – have added to the cultural *backwardness* of Catholicism an almost aristocratic incomprehension of the world of industry as well as a deep attachment to the rural community.

Let us consider the evidence provided by the figures: In 1911, when agriculture in France accounted for 45 per cent of the working population, only 27 per cent worked in industry. In 1946 the figures were 38 per cent and 28 per cent, respectively, and 34 per cent was already working in the services sector. Today, although *tertiary* industries have clearly become the dominant sector (employing 63.5 per cent of the working population), industry still employs only 30 per cent, having reached a peak of 36 per cent around 1980.

These two factors remain constant today, a fact illustrated by the two following viewpoints. The first dates from the beginning of the century and highlights political suspicions about industrial progress. The second, more recent, provides a comment on the collectivist psychology of the French.

1 Jules Meline (1838–1925), actor, much-quoted author, President of the council and Minister for Agriculture – and above all a fierce protectionist – stated categorically 'however prosperous these two industries [electricity and cars] now may be, it would be a grave misconception to believe that they will continue their current development. It is obvious that a period of mass production will soon be at hand!' Increasing competitions, in his view, would have very serious implications for the status of workers in these industries.
2 Jean-Marcel Jeannenay pointed out more recently that 'most French nationals come from peasant stock, others descend from the bourgeois class [always very keen on obtaining royal office] and just a few come from the nobility'. This last group could not dedicate themselves to business pursuits without losing their status. In the nineteenth century the educated

populace became lawyers, solicitors, doctors, magistrates, officers and civil servants. They were very typically the product of the bourgeois class.

The sense of honour in being able to serve the state, to protect 'the widow and the orphan' as it was described,[4] and the desire to serve one's fellow men were most strongly felt in France from the time of Louis XIV onwards. However, this was at the expense of productive endeavour in the economic sphere.[5]

If we are to believe the historian E. Todd,[2] however, there are anthropological roots which go even deeper that the religious influences. These are linked to the structure of the French family unit and it is from this structure that key religious and political ideologies originated and indeed the particular form of economic development seen in France. Todd's perspective is of great value in exploring cross-cultural issues.

Applying his model across Europe as a whole, we can detect two distinct types of family unit structure. The 'extended', cohesive family, authoritarian and inegalitarian, leads to members remaining attached to their land and, thus, to an accumulation of family-centred material wealth (*patrimoine*) and socio-cultural heritage. The 'extended family' is in evidence in Germany, Austria and in Switzerland and some northern countries. The 'nuclear' family, on the other hand, encourages individualism and the early separation of children from their parents.

This second social structure contains two sub-types. The smallest 'nuclear' family unit is most visible in the English context. This was in evidence from the first period of industrialization and may have been instrumental in encouraging more extensive social change. For example, this structure encouraged the rapid migration towards urban and industrial centres and the taking of entrepreneurial risks outside the sphere of influence of the family.

Then there is another type of nuclear family more egalitarian in nature, typically found in Northern France, Central Spain, Portugal and Southern Italy. In the case of France, this structure combines a liberal parent–child relationship which favours the emancipation of the children and a more egalitarian approach to the transfer of inherited wealth.

The family unit, through its nature, can obviously exert an influence on the wider society of which it is part and on industry as a specific social artefact which is significant. Work patterns and managerial approaches can mirror family moves and structures. Equally obviously, society and industrial life also can shape family behaviour.

The place of the state

The historian Marc Bloch once said that 'in France the State preceded society'. By this he meant that, unlike in other nations (Germany for example), where the unifying force of language and culture preceded the setting-up of a political structure, in France it was the state which, making use of its educational system in particular produced the French 'nation'. Indeed, in France up to the seventeenth century there was neither linguistic homogeneity nor social unity. It was the state which from this period onwards created and structured a cohesive social structure.

The second element to bear in mind when seeking to define French society is the omnipresent role of the state in the country's economy. The seeds of this interventionist – often dictatorial – tradition were already sown in the philosophy of Jean-Baptiste Colbert (1619–1683). From then onwards, throughout French history, the central place of the state was to be constantly reaffirmed. Did not Louis XIV proclaim 'L'état c'est moi' ('I am the state')? The Jacobins of the French Revolution *created* a doctrine requiring a strong centralized power which was subsequently to remain fixed in the French psyche. In 1804, by issuing the 'Code Civil' Napoléon himself had a vision of a code of law which would itself contribute to unifying society.

More recently this tradition of centralization has been maintained. At the end of the Second World War, during the restoration of the country's means of production, the state played a decisive role by financing a large part of the investments made (more than 40 per cent in the years 1947–1952). It also revitalized the primary industries in particular by nationalizing energy (EDF, GDF, mines), part of the nation's investment capital (the main deposit banks and insurance companies) and the car industry (Renault, for example).

Centralization had its parallels in a government desire to protect France's commercial interests. Hence the beginning of the Fifth Republic in 1958 brought to the fore the convergence of two national political tendencies: the Gaullist plan for French independence from overseas trade partners and the interests of the more modern French capitalists for a corporatist economy. Henceforth, the 'industrial imperative' and the French style of indicative central planning, which Charles de Gaulle defined as 'a pressing obligation', would work alongside each other.[6]

In order to modernize French industry and to compensate for the gradual loss of colonial markets, until then heavily protected, private enterprise was set the task of joining forces with the state. The precept was that 'in France the economy is planned and not left to market forces'. In this endeavour varying degrees of success have come as well as the most bitter failures.

Modernization of industry

It was from the start of the Fifth Economic Plan (1965–1970), and especially during the Sixth, that France really began the process of modernization. Whatever the political persuasions of the government of the time, these changes took place as a result of the intervention of the 'state' which encouraged groupings and mergers of large industrial concerns at international level, in both the public and private sectors:

- In the steel industry: Wendel-Sidélor and Usinor (1966)
- In metallurgy: Ugine-Kulhman (1965) and then PUK (1971)
- In the aeronautical industry: Aerospatiale, Dassault and SNIAS
- In the petroleum industry: Elf-Erap
- In the car industry Peugeot–Citroën
- In the food industry BSN–Gervais–Danone

However, the resultant French conglomerates were still smaller than their foreign competitors and family businesses continued to play a significant role in manufacturing (e.g. Michelin) and in mass marketed consumer products.

The past 10 years have been characterized by the internationalization of the economy, a significant reshaping of the country's means of production and steps towards creating a viable European Community of Europe. In order to understand the behaviour of France's business community in the face of international competition it is important to identify what became of this original economic policy.

A number of the projects created under the Fifth and Sixth plans have stood the test of time – the project which led to successful developments in the railways (including the TGV), for example. In the aeronautical industry – both civil and military – and in the car industry (Renault, Peugeot–Citroën) there have been great successes. But some projects resulted in resounding failures. These include the 'Plan calcul', aimed at developing an independent French information technology base, and the 'plan machine-outil', which aimed to protect industries in decline such as steel and textiles.

Several factors explain the partial success of the state-driven economic plan. Particularly worth noting are, first, the government's overly bureaucratic and technocratic approach to economic development and, second, recent growth in preferential public procurement. In addition, the Plans had relied on three key factors:

1 Centrally administered financing – i.e. loans to companies at special rates. This in fact led to the transfer of private capital to unproductive investment in state-controlled industry.
2 Intervention in specific high-risk business sectors for both longer projects (space projects, for example) and the plans aimed at saving difficult industries such as steel and textiles.
3 The policy of maintaining public control of the commanding heights of the economy as an ideological imperative, whatever its economic merit.

Problems now also exist for state-run industry as a result of France's budgetary deficit to the point where the Balladur government is beginning its sell-off plan. European integration also restricts the level of assistance the state can provide to reduce the extent of the indebtedness of state companies. Furthermore, global markets have developed which rely on the rapid turnover of capital, goods, services and know-how (research and development) and which in fact, negate protectionist stances by government.

In spite of an increase in the number of privatizations in the mid-1980s, and the Balladur plan to reprivatize in the 1990s, today's political and economic climate is still characterized by Mitterand's 'mixed economy' and the rejection of extreme liberalism. Even if the state is no longer the provider of old, its special relationship with the country's business community is not called into question. Hence the role of 'strategic planner' – 'helping others to do rather than doing' (according to Dominique Strauss-Kahn, minister for industry and commerce, October 1992) – laid down for the state in the Eleventh Plan. But the state would still take on long-term commitment projects where private investors would be deterred by the problem of not obtaining adequate, immediate returns on investments. It would still intervene where the obsolescence of products was so rapid that it was no longer possible to await the response of the markets to justify further investment in research and development. Finally, it would still act to retain the country's expertise.

The trade unions: a spent force

Apart from the period before 1914, when so-called 'anarcho-unionism' was apolitical and aimed at eliminating state intervention in commercial/industrial activities,[7] the trade unions themselves have always involved the state and its representatives (politicians, mayors, prefects) in the resolution of labour conflicts.[8] Indeed, both French management and working classes are closely linked to the state, all the more so since they are characterized by a lack of cohesion within each group. Unlike in other countries, such as Germany, the French working class is built on the basis of horizontal stratification with widely diverse and geographically extended membership. There have also been significant patterns of change in the membership over time.[9]

In addition, with very few exceptions, French unions were industry- rather than trade-based, that is, they brought together all workers, regardless of their specialism, who contributed to the manufacture of a particular product. Trade-based unions are traditionally more united because members are recruited from a more closely knit community based on the systems of apprenticeship and the acquisition of skills which bring together those in the same trade.[7]

These central characteristics of French industrial relations were patterned by the radicalism of management and unions, on the one hand, and by the activity of the state as permanent referee, on the other. They are still in evidence today and all the elements remain interlinked. Radicalism exists because there is chronic weakness and division within the organizations of both workers and employers. The heavy interventionist policy of the state has been consistently one which has sought to head off any confrontation between them.

Today, in spite of legislation from the early 1980s aimed at regenerating industrial relations and ensuring that decision making in contracts of employment became increasingly decentralized, French management/employee relations have reached stalemate. By putting forward numerous initiatives to involve the workforce more directly in the running of the business, French management has effectively weakened the union movement.

Currently, the unionized workforce in France has fallen to between 8 per cent and 10 per cent of the working population, the lowest level among OECD countries. However, parallel with this decline, management organizations have not put forward any kind of long-term macro plans such as were produced in the 1970s. We are witnessing not a gradual retraction of state intervention but rather a move to more focused protective activities, such as the intervention which took place in 1992 to reduce the impact of large-scale redundancies.

Changes in the pattern of French industry

French business has long been noted for the interesting make-up of its industrial fabric. In 1987 the largest companies (more than 500 employees) and those with the most political weight employed 47 per cent of the manufacturing workforce and produced 60 per cent of its turnover. They also accounted for 75 per cent of exports and two-thirds of investment in the relevant sector. In spite of their low numbers, they nevertheless constituted the core of French industry. However, over the 1980s their workforce was reduced by 40 per cent. The small and medium-sized companies (SMEs), for the most part originally family businesses (0–499 employees), comprised 53 per cent of the workforce in industry in 1989 as against 42 per cent in 1980. This may explain why their actual and potential contribution to job creation has been so emphasized in France. However, this observation should not be overstated. First, the majority of these organizations are extremely small, with nine or ten employees. It is even thought that one of France's main weaknesses in relation to its principal competitors is the small number of larger SMEs. Second, the increase in numbers of SMEs and their contri-

Table 4.1 *Economic activity by industry sector in France, Germany and the UK (percentage changes 1975–1990)*

France	1975	1980	1990
Agriculture	5.8	4.6	3.7
Energy	4.0	4.3	4.0
Manufacturing Industry	27.0	25.1	21.7
Construction	8.1	7.5	5.4
Services	55.1	58.5	65.2
Germany	1975	1980	1990
Agriculture	2.8	2.1	1.5
Energy	3.7	3.4	3.0
Manufacturing Industry	34.5	31.8	32.4
Construction	6.1	6.4	5.2
Services	52.9	56.3	57.9
United Kingdom	1975	1980	1990
Agriculture	2.8	2.1	1.4
Energy	6.1	10.1	5.7
Manufacturing Industry	28.7	27.0	20.9
Construction	6.5	6.2	5.2
Services	55.9	54.6	66.8

Sources: Comptes nationaux – INSEE, OCDE.

bution is, in turn, largely explained by the recent and rapid restructuring of France's means of production. In effect, several large companies came into the category of SMEs in the 1980s after privatizations, followed by extensive redundancies, outsourcing and decentralizing many operations branches.

France, like all other European countries, has been struggling in the past three years with the problem of loss of competitiveness in many of its core industry sectors. Privatization in the 1980s was aimed at arresting decline in market shares. As elsewhere, there is evidence of a long-term trend in France towards extensive de-industrialization. This can be observed in both the purely economic sphere – manufacturing industry represents 22 per cent of GDP in 1990 against 27 per cent in 1975 (see Table 4.1) – and in the employment figures. Industry lost a quarter of its workforce, or more than 100 000 jobs per year, between 1975 and 1990. Among France's trading partners only the UK experienced such a decline. Japanese and German industry suffered less from the effects of the crisis in manufacturing.

As elsewhere, also, France witnessed an expansion of the tertiary sector,

Table 4.2 *Employment in France by economic activity sectors*

	Number (thousands) 1990	1990 (%)
Agriculture, forestry, fishing	1 339.1	6.0
Food Industries	571.7	2.6
Energy	240.8	1.1
Intermediate Manufacture	1 232.1	5.6
Original Equipment Manufacture	1 505.6	6.8
Consumer Goods Manufacture	1 168.2	5.3
Building, Civil Engineering	1 600.0	7.2
Commerce	2 734.3	12.4
Transport and Telecommunications	1 292.3	5.8
Wholesale and Retail	4 875.0	22.0
Other Services	5 581.0	25.2
Total	22 140.1	100.0

Source: INSEE Tableaux de l'Economie française 1991–1992.

to the extent that the service industries outweigh manufacturing industry in levels of employment and added-value, whereas it represented only 50 per cent in 1970. Today this growth is mainly due to the significant development in the services-to-industry sector, whether in 'know-how' (information technology and management consultancy, accounting or marketing consultancy) or in the outsourcing of auxiliary functions (such as temporary work, transport maintenance) and, to a lesser extent, in services to individuals (health, private hospital treatment, radio, television, for example).

An overview of the distribution of jobs in the French economy is illustrated in Table 4.2. In addition to the figures listed in the table, civil servants comprise 18.6 per cent of the working population and the public sector (as defined by such statistics as the number of employees, gross income and return on investment) is 18 per cent of the country's income (against 11 per cent in Germany, 19.5 per cent in Italy, 5.5 per cent in the UK and an average of 12.6 per cent across the EU).

Difficulties encountered in adapting to meet international competition

To tackle these issues, investment within each sector has definitely increased overall since 1984 but it is still unstable (falling once again in 1990) and generally insufficient. These investments currently represent 20 per cent of the GDP, which is the average across the twelve EU countries, as against

23.5 per cent in Germany and 30 per cent in Japan. This is partly explained by the relatively high level of borrowing, particularly among French SMEs.

Similarly, investment in research represents a significant long-term key to successful future development. France is in fourth place in levels of expenditure on research and development, with 2.4 per cent of GDP. Only Japan, the United States and Germany are ahead in this area. The UK and Italy are way behind. France is ahead even of the United States and Germany in the level of annual increase in spending which in 1991 reached 4.6 per cent of GDP against 4.5 per cent and 4.2 per cent in the previously mentioned countries. It should be noted, however, that these overall figures hide a significant imbalance. Only six areas of industrial activity (aeronautical, electronics, automotive, chemical, pharmaceutical and energy) account for three-quarters of the total investment in research and development. Construction, public works, mechanical engineering and textiles are regularly 'forgotten'. Also, 6 per cent of the largest companies take 75 per cent of the capital invested. The majority of the SMEs – unlike in Germany – see little of these funds.

It is not the intention of this section to deal with the national debate on the effects of 'competitive deflation/disinflation' which was the policy selected by the socialist governments to improve France's competitive position in the late 1980s nor will the issue of global competition be considered here, as this will be addressed later.

Without entering into too much detail and avoiding undue emphasis on current issues we provide here a rough outline of the key features and the short-, medium- and long-term developments of the means of production in France. The industrial sector will be considered in more detail as experts agree upon the significance this sector plays in the search for French competitiveness.

Overall, in 1994, the image of a French industry which is highly introverted most definitely belongs to the past. It is true that not all companies have shared to the same extent in the globalization of markets and the world-scale restructuring of industrial production units. Many organizations have forged ahead, such as Michelin, Alcatel-Alsthom, BSN, Saint-Gobain, ELF-Aquitaine and Air Liquide. Others again experienced difficulties in adapting in recent years and yet others have been able to keep up the pace thanks only to state assistance, such as Renault, Pechiney, Usinor-Sacilor and Rhône-Poulenc. Indeed, as a result of competitor pressures and the European recession, the business failure rate in France reached an all-time high in 1991, at a level 60 per cent above the average of industrialized countries. Moreover, there has not been a sufficiently high level of creation of companies to compensate for this. Indeed, company formation, too, has been in decline.

In contrast, two factors which contribute to long- and short-term competitiveness in France are particularly worth noting:

Table 4.3 *Labour costs in manufacturing industry (hourly earnings and fringe benefits in US dollars)*

	1970	1975	1980	1985	1989	1990
Germany	2.58	6.37	12.89	10.08	19.00	23.44
France	1.77	4.61	9.56	7.78	12.78	15.87
Italy	1.90	4.48	9.64	8.20	15.27	18.45
UK	1.61	3.45	7.32	6.63	12.83	15.30
Spain	0.84	–	6.43	5.48	10.69	13.54
Netherlands	2.19	6.55	12.79	8.81	15.44	18.79
USA	4.33	6.54	10.04	13.09	14.40	14.96
Japan	1.08	3.37	6.80	8.03	15.78	16.00

Source: National statistics; author's calculations.

Table 4.4 *Output per hour in manufacturing industry (percentage change, annual average or year to year)*

	1971/1975	1981/1985	1990
Germany	4.8	2.8	3.5
France	4.4	3.7	1.0
Italy	4.3	5.1	3.2
UK	3.4	5.6	0.8

1 A significant drop in the cost of manpower, which places the average hourly wage in France 25 per cent lower than in Germany (see Table 4.3).
2 A policy of continuous training and development which has become part of an overall strategy and is prioritized within large organizations, with an average of 3.2 per cent of overall expenditure on manpower in 1991.

These factors combine with a good level of general productivity, where gains have always been higher than those of France's main competitors. In the period 1979–1989 the figure was 2.1 per cent per year as against Germany's 1.6 per cent and 1 per cent in the United States. Only Japan was ahead with 3 per cent.

Strengths and weaknesses in the main sectors

It is difficult to identify the main sectors that contribute to France's competitiveness in the way we can identify mechanical engineering and electronics in Japan. However, it is possible to define the French economy, focusing on strengths and weaknesses.

Today, France is the world's fourth-largest exporting nation and the third-largest investor worldwide. It is particularly active in Europe and in commercial services (banks, insurance, etc.). A financial capitalism is becoming established which is more dynamic than the earlier industrial capitalism. There is also a substantial increase in inbound investment in the services sector. However, France has for a long time struggled to maintain its trade balance.

France does have a number of trump cards but these are spread across a range of sectors. Agriculture, banking, insurance and tourism play a part in French competitiveness. However, the key sectors are agribusiness (where the surplus has increased fivefold since 1980), aeronautical and defence. Space alone is currently showing 7 per cent growth annually. The car industry accounts for 11 per cent of total manufacturing output, although it is a highly vulnerable sector which lost 30 per cent of its workforce between 1978 and 1990. The chemical industries (ranked fourth worldwide) and lastly, telecommunications represent the key sectors for French competitiveness.

It is particularly the medium-sized firms that have difficulties in exporting, especially in the capital goods sector. Most notably, the mechanical engineering industry, although employing 11.3 per cent of France's industrial workforce (i.e. 440 000 employees), cannot keep pace with its competitors. This is particularly so in the case of machine-tool production, in spite of recent efforts towards modernization. The sector is made up of large numbers of small firms and has difficulties in attracting skilled labour. The sector is currently being restructured, due mainly to the efforts of large financial concerns (Financière de Valois, Legris Industrie, for instance) which are seeking to group the SMEs in the sector to increase their capacity for investment.

The textile industry should also be mentioned here. It is currently experiencing an increasing influx of foreign competitors in the domestic market and has halved its workforce during the last 20 years. France is also witnessing a decline in sales of other consumer goods such as perfumes and clothing. Lastly, one should consider the electrical/electronics sector with 455 000 employees or 12 per cent of the industrial workforce. Although currently recording an overall deficit, two deeply contrasting elements are apparent. Even if the electrical industry has been highly active, having doubled production levels in 10 years, electronics and information technology in particular have experienced the same decline as in Europe as a whole. The much-publicized failures of Bull and Thompson put paid to the plan of making France the third largest producer of information technology in the world, as President Mitterrand had hoped in 1981.

Table 4.5 *Changes in professional and socio-professional work categories*

Professional groups	1962	1975	1982	1990	Change 1962–1982	Change 1982–1990
Agricultural workers	15.9	7.8	6.3	5.0	–3.6	–2.9
Artisans, business executives						
heads of companies	10.9	8.1	7.8	8.0	–0.6	–0.5
Managers and higher						
intellectual professions	4.6	7.1	8.1	11.6	+3.8	+3.2
Intermediate professions	11.0	16.0	16.9	20.1	+3.2	+1.3
White-collar employees	18.4	23.4	26.5	26.1	+2.9	+1.7
Blue-collar employees	39.0	37.3	32.9	28.1	+0.2	–0.8
Unemployed	1.1	4.1	8.1	9.2		
Active working population	100.0	100.0	100.0	100.0		

Source: INSEE.

The restructuring of socio-economic groups and employment

A number of social changes have accompanied the process of modernization during recent years. Only the most salient features are discussed here.

First, a change in the pattern of work and the distribution of jobs since 1962 has brought about a progressive reduction in opportunities for employment in agriculture and in small businesses for skilled and unskilled labour. In the case of agriculture this gradual reduction is not simply an issue of retraining. It represents a move away from the roots of the country as a whole. As for small businesses, they have been less resistant to change than craftsmen.

For the skilled and unskilled workforce there are two points to add: it is the lowest qualified groups that have experienced the fastest drop in numbers employed (4.1 per cent per year between 1974 and 1980 and 6 per cent per year 1980–1990). Employees in general are in the same position, the number of workers dropping by 8.1 million between 1975 and 1990.

The increase in the numbers in management between 1962 and 1990 has been steady, with the total doubling in 20 years. However, this increase is mainly in general management, whereas in engineering the increase began to slow down from 1980. Unskilled workers in this sector were also affected (see Table 4.5). The total working population is 24.8 million or 43 per cent of the total population in 1992, as against 16.2 per cent retired.

In the search for greater competitive flexibility in production, which particularly affected the workforce at the beginning of the 1980s, the number of different types of employment contract increased, radically altering traditional patterns. Currently it is estimated that approximately 3 million people are employed under these new terms which include temporary work (209 000 or one in ten and 70 per cent men), fixed-term contracts (580 000) and more established forms of employment such as temporary contracts, apprenticeships or training placements (around 502 000 individuals).

There are also 3 million others working in part-time positions, equivalent to 12 per cent of the working population and including seven times more women than men, though few are in these positions out of choice. Even though France may be behind on the issue of flexibility in relation to countries such as the United States or the Northern countries, there would nevertheless seem to be evidence of a certain degree of potential flexibility. However, this flexibility has been used politically for the purposes of diffusing any potential social tensions and as a defensive measure against unemployment, rather than as a long-term economic solution.

On the issue of changes in the labour market, the unprecedented increase in numbers of female workers over the last 20 years should also be noted. During this period their numbers increased by 3 million, as opposed to an increase of less than 1 million among male workers, and reached 42 per cent of the working population in 1990.

With the problems in adjusting to these changes in supply and demand in the labour market, with approximately 10 per cent unemployed, France is in an unenviable position in relation to other industrialized nations. The nature of the categories of unemployed is particularly interesting: a large number of young people (around 25 per cent of active 15–24-year-olds) are out of work. There are 12.8 per cent of women unemployed as opposed to 7.9 per cent of men, double the number of immigrants as opposed to native French, and also significant regional imbalances.

During the past two years two further factors have emerged as important in addition to those already mentioned: an increase in the time spent unemployed and a sharp rise in the number of unemployed managers. Until recently this group had been sheltered, but in 1990 this rose by 12 per cent and in 1991 by 34 per cent. In spite of strong welfare support and several hundred thousand taking early retirement, insurance companies and the provision of state social security are under severe pressure.

In order to tackle the problem of the young unemployed, there needs to be improved cooperation/links between the education system and the world of business. Educational reforms are now required. The German system of 'dual' training could be used as a model. However, the question arises as to whether the vocational training channels (technical and professional) could regain the value they once had, having long been neglected and ignored.

The legal and institutional framework

It is the very foundations of French society which are today being called into question by the need for France to sharpen its commercial edge. In almost every area they are found wanting in the face of the challenges they face. The three most important challenges which need to be urgently addressed are:

- Reforms in the education system
- The development of new forms of support for the unemployed and new unemployment schemes
- Updating of employer/employee relations and of industrial relations structures.

The education system

The French education system is said to be elitist, inegalitarian, discriminatory, exclusive and to promote a split between the different education channels. The system encourages the acquisition of theoretical knowledge with a selection process which is based purely on performance in mathematics. This is often seen as a large uncontrollable machine and the main criticism levied against it is that general education is given priority at the expense of more technical, and that vocational training is seen as a last resort.

Therefore, although France has the highest number of students going on to higher education (degree level) within the EU – 15.4 per cent according to OECD figures – in fact only 200 000 students per year receive vocational training. In Germany the figure is 1 500 000. In addition, 300 000 – or 30 per cent of a year's intake of pupils – leave school each year without any qualifications. Another relevant symptom is that the CAP (*Certificat d'Aptitude Professionnelle*), the first step towards qualification for blue-collar workers, is increasingly being abandoned, especially in the training colleges, where the number of pupils taking the certificate dropped from 430 000 in 1980 to 85 000 in 1991. It is true that another training route – the CFA (*Centre de Formation d'Apprentissage*) – saw its numbers stabilize at 200 000 per year. Students who receive basic professional training amount to 300 000 in total, a low figure when compared with their German counterparts, who are five times more numerous.

Two additional factors affect this poor training. There is the persistent inability to adapt the specialist courses offered to the requirements of the market. Secretarial, hairdressing and bakery courses, for example, are chosen in preference to the such badly needed manufacturing skills in construction, forge and boiler making. There is also an abnormally high discrepancy of 60 per cent between the numbers who start the CAP courses and those who achieve a qualification.

Efforts have certainly been made over the last decade to remedy these deficiencies. Those often quoted are the IUT (Institut Universitaire de Technologie) in higher-level technical training. At a lower level two new Baccalauréats have been created. The Baccalauréat Professionnel was set up in 1985, and was followed by the Baccalauréat Technologique aimed at making trainees immediately employable either at supervisory, technical or management level or as highly skilled workers. Without going into more detail, it would seem that most students who follow these courses of study are keen to continue them. This means that students move on to higher qualifications which, unfortunately, do not meet the requirements of industry. At the same time, the business world complains of a lack of suitably qualified workers.

These factors are present at all levels: among the young technicians who are more attracted to research and working methods than by production and among trainee engineers who prefer research to workshops and production.

We have not paid sufficient attention to the fact that many of the shortcomings of the French education system are the direct result of its deeply equalitarian philosophy. By proclaiming 'secondary and university education for all' and aiming for '80 per cent of a given age group reaching Baccalauréat level' the system has constantly supported the prestige attached to a high-level formal academic education and the rejection of the more vocational channels which, until now, have been less sought after in the labour market.

However, several aspects of the system are currently under consideration.[10] First, there is the improvement in training of the workers, which is fundamentally important for productivity. This has been neglected for far too long by a country which has been suffering a scarcity of manpower. These improvements could take the form of on-the-job training and the setting up of apprenticeships, a form of training little used until recently in French industry.

However, companies themselves should also take on some responsibility for training by making jobs more challenging, by providing training and development programmes and career management for the workers. The education system for its part should move towards a more decentralized structure, more open and moving away from the previous system. Without doubt, a challenging task!

Changes in job structures – job sharing

Another approach involves changing current working structures in order to protect jobs. This balancing is a relatively recent phenomenon and brings to the fore the issue of new ways of preventing further unemployment within

the labour market. Until the mid-1980s the majority of French decision makers
had believed that the modernization of a company and plans for dealing
with the recession would be mainly achieved through technical innovation.
By undertaking a relatively ambitious investment programme in this area
they all too often overlooked the human capacity for adapting to change,
the changes required within the organization e.g. the structure of qualification requirements and the management styles which had to accompany the
introduction of new technologies.[11]

As a result, the 1980s were most notable for the significant restructuring
within industry, massive redundancy and early retirement programmes,
social planning and, occasionally, for whole programmes which consisted
of substituting the existing workforce (considered to be no longer suitable)
with younger and better-trained workers. In other words, the employment
structures themselves were considered to be a method of adjustment to the
market rather than understanding their fundamental importance, and the
nature of a job was changed before the people involved could change and
adapt.

This explains the recent increase in specific types of employment contracts in France such as fixed-term contracts, compulsory part-time working
and temporary staff. In the guise of increasing flexibility, these have in fact
contributed to weakening the previous relationships between employer and
employee. Whereas between 1970 and 1975 these types of contract were
considered unusual and accounted for 3.2 million people in a working
population of 22.5 million, between 1982 and 1990 the figures were 5 million out of a total of 24.5 million, or more than 20 per cent. Similarly, open
contracts and long-term employment, the norm in 1975, accounted for 80
per cent of all contracts of employment. This fell to 65 per cent in 1990.[12]

In order to guard against the dangers of a two-speed economy and the
increasing pressure on the more vulnerable groups within the working
population, a number of legislative measures were taken and structures for
providing assistance were set up by the Ministry for Employment. These
were aimed at encouraging companies to see themselves more as 'learning
organizations', more flexible and more open with restructuring of tasks,
and reductions in the numbers of levels within the company hierarchies
and career planning. Work should be more stimulating and varied, the
management of personnel and their training should be proactive and efforts
should be made to support the less-qualified sectors of the population to
limit the effects on society at large of an overly-hurried deregulation.

These were the aims laid down for the 'Engagements de Développement
et de la Formation' (a state organization for the development of training),
Training Conventions, the 'Fonds pour l'Amélioration des Conditions de
Travail' (provisions for the improvement of terms of employment), the 'Aide
au Conseil' (advisory service for employment) and the Mission 'Nouvelles

Table 4.6 *Changes in the number of French trade union representatives, 1985–1989*

Union	Number of union representatives		
	1985 (amended)	1987	1989
CGT	13 590	12 753	11 930
CFDT	11 000	10 602	10 200
CGT-FO	7 894	7 967	7 674
CFE-CGC	6 073	6 086	5 625
CFTC	3 027	3 196	3 124
Other unions	2 687	2 774	2 907
Total	44 271	43 378	41 460

Source: *Employment Statistics*, No. 68, April 1991.

Qualifications' (a national training plan). The most extreme measure was taken at the end of 1992. This obliged companies contemplating redundancies to put forward a structured plan which was then closely monitored by the authorities.

However, the solutions implemented until recently have already revealed their limitations. Faced with the combined problems of the welfare state and the social security system, both of which are in crisis, the issue of a genuine sharing of work is being considered, starting with a reduction in working hours. The 1981 government initiative to move from a 40-hour week to 39 hours failed as it was considered too sweeping. An alternative presented itself: an experiment with more precisely targeted actions. This would, however, require a profound transformation in French industrial relations. However, in this area a number of problems were encountered.

Modernizing the structures for collective bargaining

It has been seen that French employer/employee relations have been shaped by a number of historical constants which are highly influential. These could be summarized as follows:

1 A relatively weak and splintered union movement based on militant politics. To judge by the figures in Table 4.6, for the most typical unions, the movement is in the process of deteriorating. Its history is marked by schism and fighting between unions in the same sector. However, there are also short periods of association, of attempts at revising political stances and unification between groups, the details of which are far too complex to be fully explained here.[13]
2 The lack of a cohesive coordinated representative organization for owners.

France is a country where large companies with a low level of industrial concentration co-exist with large numbers of independent small and medium-sized enterprises. Management is constantly threatened by problems which vary widely according in a given industry to the size of organization, e.g. between the GGPME (Confédération Générale des Petites et Moyennes Entreprises), the National Federation of Small and Medium-sized Companies and the CNPF representing the larger companies. Ideological divisions in the ranks prevent a concerted view between the more progressive generators of new ideas such as the CJD, ETHIC, and 'Entreprise et Progrès' (an association for business development) and the more conventional (e.g. CNPF). Again divisions are possible according to the type of organization, i.e. between confederal associations covering a range of industries such as the CNPF and sector-specific associations such as UIMM (Union of Metallurgical and Mining Industries). In other words, no collective employers' organization exists which is 'capable of creating a spirit of unity or exerting a genuine social authority'.[9] This results in policies which place independence of a company above its successful development. Shareholders, being protectionist by tradition, are more receptive to management agreements with competitors than to taking risks in the marketplace.[14] Reynaud[7] notes that French management is safety-concious and precise, and, in addition, has always favoured a policy of neutralization of the powers of the unions.

3 An industrial relations structure which is openly confrontational, litigious and centralized. The logic is one of provocative tactics on the part of the unions and a policy of problem-avoidance from the management, rather than one of negotiation. The structure is bureaucratic, as it is strictly codified, with the written laws having significant influence over contractual agreements. It is centralized in that, before the belated sectionalization of the unions by industry and by companies (1968), the state was more or less fully guaranteed to undertake the role of arbitrator in situations of conflict at national and branch level and across different industry sectors.

The system now relies on bodies representing employees which have only limited and essentially consultative powers, and are complex and confusing in their structures. The best known are the 'Délégué du Personnel' (individuals within each company elected to represent the workforce) set up in 1946 with the aim of 'presenting/supporting individual or collective claims relating to salaries and to ensure the application of the 'Codes du Travail' (Employment Laws) and legislation concerning social security, health and safety and collective decisions or agreements applicable within the labour market (Code du Travail, article L-422–1) and the 'Comité d'Entreprise' which emerged in 1945. The latter's concerns are 'socio-cultural activities', in which it has a genuine decision-making role, and in business management where its role is more that of generation of ideas, of supervision or consultancy rather than having decision-making powers. This distinguishes it from the German *Mitbestimmung* structure for involving employees in management, for example.

There are two major other institutions worth noting. First, there is the 'Conseil des Prud'hommes' (employees' tribunal) consisting of employees from various companies with responsibility for settling individual disputes relating to contracts of employment, including salaries, discipline and especially redundancy. Second is the Works Inspectorate staffed by civil servants who monitor companies' adherence to legislation concerning working conditions, occasionally stepping in to settle differences between opposing interests. It is interesting to note that the first dates from Napoleonic times.

During the gradual build-up of this edifice, however, the unions in France secured the possibility of negotiation with employers only at a very late stage (1968). Previously employers negotiated only at either a national and regional inter-professional level and outside the company itself. Two structures (the Délégué du Personnel and the Comité d'Entreprise) acted as the only channels of communication with militant unionists. At the end of the 1970s an important change began to take place in the system which until then had been relatively stable. With the first tremors of the recession being felt, reductions in mass production and the search for greater productivity, management began increasingly to take the lead and to dominate industrial relations. In order to introduce more flexible production, it was necessary also to have a more flexible salary structure, a reduction in national insurance contributions – which weighed heavily on companies – and a slackening of the legal constraints relating to the employment laws.

It was, therefore, the very foundations of the system which were and are still being re-examined. The emergence of the concept of individually negotiated salaries is of special significance. On the one hand, it deals a hefty blow at the time-honoured system of bureaucratic classifications of positions which had gradually been built up over the years by the combined efforts of employers and unions. On the other, it demonstrates that this development could, in fact, stand in the way of a restructuring of jobs and of competency-based qualifications.

Faced with this desire for deregulation, France legislated. There was the historic Act of 1971 introducing what was almost a legal obligation for employers to devote a part of their salary budget (currently 1.2 per cent, soon to move up to 1.4 per cent) to ongoing training of employees. Then came the Auroux Laws of 1982, which sought to reactivate industrial relations by employees' rights to direct and individual expression on given issues such as conditions of employment and job descriptions, together with a right to the yearly renegotiation of salaries.

However, the effects of this initiative on the decline of the unions were

Table 4.7 *Collective agreements by size of business or organization*

Size of organization	Organizations using collective agreements (%)		Employees covered under collective agreements (%)	
	1981	*1985*	*1981*	*1985*
10–49 employees	7.7	14.8	8.0	15.4
50–199 employees	15.8	25.9	15.7	27.8
200–499 employees	29.5	45.0	29.1	46.0
500-plus	44.7	63.8	51.5	68.7
All sizes	9.9	17.7	24.2	35.4

Source: Annual Collective Negotiations 1985.

considerably reduced by, among other factors, the segmentation of the blue-collar worker groups and, at the same time, the development of new management techniques and direct involvement of the workforce (for example, in quality circles, participative and project management). Although many agreements were signed, the active use of 'discussion groups' was far from being universal. It has not met the expectations of the state nor the requirements of many unions and employer groups.

The current situation, paradoxically, is that, while the business world has recently received a better press from public opinion in general, there can be shown to have taken place a gradual retreat from the usual forum for negotiation on the part of management and workforce. Of course, negotiation on the issue of salaries, including social security and training, still takes place at the national level. However, the general tendency is towards decentralization and a vast number of company-specific agreements have emerged (Renault, Usinor-Sacilor, Gan, Axa). It is these which constitute the latest policy in the move to modernization as far as the weakening of the unions is concerned.

From now on, it is at company level that decisions on industrial relations will be made, both on the issue of salaries and on the quantitative/qualitative changes required within the workforce to meet the changing needs of the market. (These constituted 10 per cent of subjects for debate in 1991.) Admittedly, these changes have taken place mainly within large companies (see Table 4.7) predominantly within industry (60 per cent) rather than in the service sector (36 per cent), and within only a few business sectors (bulk chemicals and electrical engineering). In addition, the changes have been largely restricted to areas either identified a long time ago as key issues – salaries accounted for over half the agreements reached in 1991 and profit sharing, 9824 agreements affecting 1.9 million beneficiaries – or decided by general consensus (the issue of training).

A number of these company-specific initiatives are almost experimental, such as those which focus on the job and salary sharing and which have resulted in agreements between management and labour on reductions in both working hours and pay (CIC-Bordeaux, MAAF, Montabert, Biscuiterie Nantaise, Potain etc.). These innovations are still rather ambivalent. On the one hand, they could be seen as retrograde steps, threatening once again the benefits secured. On the other, they may indicate the emergence of new forms of welfare protection which are more directly accessible, away from the great mechanism of the state benefits system. However, in a country where industrial relations were never totally left to be dictated by market forces and where the containment of the workforce has never been especially effective, opportunities for progress are limited.

The principal features of the French style of management

Within the context described, an attempt will be made to study the key characteristics of French management. Some are common to all forms of management (for example, the emphasis on technology, the awareness of management styles). Others apply more to larger organizations (headhunting as central recruitment policy, tendency to overly bureaucratic structure, emphasis on human resource management) or to SMEs (the avoidance – if not the repression – of union activity). Without claiming to be exhaustive, the following review highlights the similarities and differences.

A range of different management cultures

In France it is not only the political authorities which seek to mitigate the effects of pure competition. Given that ownership of capital was never considered to imply legitimate power and that there was always a tension in the ownership of the means of production, the distribution of profits has always been particularly sharply debated. French management in general has, for the most part, always been inclined to seek the help of the state as direct or indirect referee. However, there are several types of management in France, corresponding very closely to the different types of company. Broadly, these are divided according to numbers of employees as follows:[16]

1 The management of very small companies, which are in fact the majority. Indeed, 93.5 per cent of French companies consist of less than 10 employees, accounting for 22 per cent of the labour force, of which only 7 per cent are in manufacturing. This first type of management is artisanal, highly self-reliant and resistant to state help, though with relatively limited economic influence.

2 The management of SMEs (10–499 employees) which represent 6.9 per cent of French companies, employing 42 per cent of the workforce, but accounting for 46 per cent of manufacturing industry. This owner-manager group is protectionist, Malthusian and paternalistic. Above all, it is keen to maintain its independence and to transfer its wealth to its successors. As Weber[1] stated: 'Fearing nothing so much as taking risks, be it from competition, innovation or excessively rapid expansion of the company, this management group is forced to defend its market share by seeking the guidance under the protective wing of the state.'

3 In addition, there is, of course, a group of entrepreneurial managers which is identifiable not so much by the size of the organizations to which it belongs but by the individual routes to personal development and the way they achieved their current positions, the latter being the result of their own endeavours and of having promoted a corporate *laissez-faire* culture of maximizing productivity within a spirit of management by consensus. This is the only management group which does not rely over-much on the assistance of the state.[1]

4 Lastly there is the management of large organizations. These represent 0.1 per cent of French companies but they employ 36 per cent of the workforce and account for 47 per cent of manufacturing industry. This group currently consists of between 5000 and 10 000 individuals who have considerable political power. They are typically 'professional' managers who have achieved their positions through having either technical or managerial knowledge, i.e. they were selected for their particular expertise. As in many other countries, 'hereditary' managers, or managers who inherit great capitalist dynasties, are declining in numbers, whereas this last group of large-company, professional managers is currently expanding rapidly. In addition, it is from the ranks of this group and from the group of entrepreneurial managers that are drawn the majority of the supporters of the CNPF (National Confederation of French Managers).

The training and development of senior management in France

Research published by Bauer and Bertin-Mourot[17] shows that the strongest relationships between French enterprise and state are evidenced within the largest companies. The authors compare French and German situations examining how, within the large conglomerates, the very top managers reach their positions. Three distinct types of managers are identified: the 'entrepreneur' managers who were 'spotted', recruited and trained and who may have capital resources to contribute; the 'institutionalists' with valuable political or state connections; and the 'career' managers.

The first group achieved their success either by founding companies or by building on what they inherited, taking advantage of the exploits of their predecessors (inheritors or members of one of the monied families). The second group come more or less directly from the state bodies: cabinet ministers, top civil servants and politicians. The third group owe their success to their experience and behaviour within the company. Some have earned their stripes by remaining faithful to a single company. Others have proved their worth in a variety of roles and with a number of different organizations.

The outcome of the research confirmed the trends identified within companies mentioned above. Whereas 44.5 per cent of French top management come from the second group, in Germany the figure is only 8 per cent. Furthermore, 'career' managers account for 65.5 per cent of German senior managers but only 21.8 per cent of French management reached the top ranks in this way.

Even more importantly, the nature of the academic qualification achieved and the educational establishment attended play a crucial role in the success of senior managers. Indeed, within the senior management of French parent companies there are only 16 per cent of 'self-made men and women'. There are, however, 27 per cent from the 'Polytechniques', 19 per cent are former students of the ENA (Ecole Nationale d'Administration) and 7 per cent from the HEC (Hautes Ecoles de Commerce). In other words, three business schools which between them produce 500 graduates each year turn out over 50 per cent of the 'big bosses'.[17] There is, in addition, the system of (slightly less prestigious) 'Grandes Ecoles', and the other universities which train several hundreds of thousands of students but contribute only 20 per cent and 10 per cent, respectively.

In effect, it is as if, in France, the task of selecting the country's future leaders is delegated to the education system, the destiny of these individuals themselves being predetermined by the schools they attended. This system takes 30 per cent of managers straight to the directors' chair of their chosen establishment. The alternative system, more typically German, relies predominantly on an extensive professional experience of commitment to the company and on a suitable 'apprenticeship', where the individuals in question acquire theoretical knowledge and progress rapidly up the lower echelons of the company. Such factors would seem to carry far less weight in France when seeking the highest positions of responsibility.

The origins of the management 'class' and the introduction of an intermediate career path

In France, as we have seen, there are very clear horizontal divisions within the management hierarchy, and the vertical divisions within the structure

Table 4.8 *Managers in France 1990*

	Number	‰
Engineers and technical managers	612 387	25.7
Public administrators	286 014	12.0
Teachers, Scientific professions	567 527	23.9
Professionals in communication, arts and entertainment	168 312	7.1
Administrative and commercial managers	744 516	31.3
Total	2 378 756	100.0

Source: INSEE.

of an organization are no less definite. For example, the average salary of white-collar workers is 6 per cent higher than that of the blue-collar group (as opposed to 20 per cent higher in Germany, Italy and Denmark). Un-skilled labour has been the most heavily affected by redundancies during the recession.

The divide between the different groups – management and workers – within the hierarchy is almost impossible to cross. In industry it exists immediately above the foreman level. These 'Contremaîtres – Agents de Maîtrise' or foreman are listed in the category of middle-level professions, without actually being given management status.

The status of management itself is not clearly defined. It does not relate to the job description, the level of training undertaken or the extent of responsibilities. 'Manager' is more than a professional description: the title gives a genuine social cachet. Access to manager status has long been equivalent to a form of ennoblement in the popular imagination (see Table 4.8).[18] Indeed it took a long time for lower–middle managers above the foreman level to be eventually recognized as members of the manager caste. Having now adopted its social and cultural behaviour, this group now constitutes the real core of French management as summarized by Taddie and Coriat.[19] It is worth noting that:

- Compared to its competitors France is the country with the highest numbers of managers in Europe. Managers constitute 14 per cent of all employees compared to only 9.3 per cent in Germany, the average being 12.5 per cent.
- France is the country within Europe which relies most heavily on external recruitment of managers both in percentage (76 per cent) and absolute numbers, as opposed to managers reaching the same level through internal promotion.

One cannot but wonder if the current flexibility and communication re-quirements of business and industry are not incompatible with some of the sociological rigidities implied by such a management caste system. Now, however, it seems that managers' jobs can no longer be protected. The number of unemployed managers in the year to end-1992 grew by 23.9 per cent. Faced with the problem of the cost of managers as part of the organization superstructure, employers are ensuring that jobs are becoming less specifically defined. The same phenomenon of multi-skilling is observable throughout Europe. Similarly, in many industrial sectors, a reorganization in hierarchical levels can already be observed. This delayering aims at reducing the divisions between managers and non-managers. A genuine revolution, so far as France is concerned.

The strengthening of bureaucratic trends in larger organizations in France has been another relevant feature. As early as 1963, Michel Crozier, a French sociologist, identified a strengthening of the 'bureaucratic phenomenon' in his study of the development and problems of working in large organizations.[20] Using empirical analysis of administrative and industrial organizations, he identified key relevant features as follows:

- The isolation of employees and professional groups; a large number of impersonal rules and their role in individual and collective protection.
- The lack of efficiency of the objectives decided by managers and the lack of control achieved.
- The extreme centralization of the power of decisions and the daily difficulty for employees in solving immediate problems.
- Reluctant attitudes towards changes and a process of transformation based only on sporadic crises.
- The constant presence of power. The fact that each person wants to control the greatest part of it in preference to any other form of social interaction.

In particular, Crozier noted that the excessive use of organizational rules and routines in the model of 'French bureaucracy' was a function of the aversion of French employees to direct relationships and to the control enforced by managers. Therefore it played a role of self-protection at the expense of efficiency. It is clear that even bureaucratization is now under immense threat.

Philippe d'Iribarne provides us with yet another perspective of differing managerial approaches.[21] Thanks to his empirical analysis of companies from three different countries (France, the United States and the Netherlands), the writer shows the very important differences that exist in the organization and management of these companies. According to d'Iribarne, these differences can be explained through the history of national cultures.

In the United States, the relationships between the employers and employees are based on explicit contracts and processes which define the limits and objectives of the tasks of any person in the company. In the Netherlands the running of companies is based on the constant search for a consensus between the employers and employees. However, in France the main feature is based on the attachment of each employee to his or her independence at work.

In France, the tasks of each employee are considered as an 'obligation'. He or she would naturally assume the ownership of these tasks and the rights and duties that obviously follow. This could define the hierarchical relations between managers and subordinates according almost to an implied code of obligations and honour. In such a culture, any control of an employee's work would be an affront to his or her dignity. It would cut across the 'code of honour'. Moreover, the fact that some tasks are considered as 'obligations' would/could explain the great number of hierarchical levels and the compartmentalization of French companies. 'France is a society based on ranks' declared d'Iribane. The managerial ranks follow a medieval hierarchy from less 'noble' to more 'noble' in a league-table fashion. Such an unwritten code contributes much to the feeling of structured authoritarianism in French business and the panoply of arrangements with which people protect their independence.

The conclusions of d'Iribane's research indicate that the management methods – particularly those that consist of managing managers – cannot work without insight into cultural 'rules'. As a consequence, it is almost impossible – in his view – to transfer a cultural model from one country to another. However, one of the challenges that French management could accept would consist of drawing inspiration from the principles of 'post-industrial' management, as developed in the United States or in Japan. These principles could then be adopted to the socio-cultural values of France. According to the writer, this could be possible but particularly ambitious.

The priority given to the modernization of technology

A key element that requires highlighting is the long-standing prevalence of a technocratic culture in French management. Indeed, for a long time the production engineer or the technician-manager had such a key position in French industry that it was said that French management is, on the whole, based more on technological than on management skills, more enthused with technical exploits than commercial feats.

For instance, in the car industry Citroën has a tradition of inventiveness. It illustrates amply the French model of the prevalence of research departments over everything else. It does not matter if the engineers ignore the industrialization problems and fashion! It does not matter if the process of development is too long (as it was in the launch of the well-known 2CV in 1949), so long as the technologist's vision prevails.

Even some of the concepts of modernization that have appeared in France during recent years confirm this analysis. At the end of the 1970s and at the beginning of the 1980s the change in the productive system in France was achieved through the use of new technologies (e.g. IT, production engineering). For many, it was a period of inflexible authorization where the technicalities of production, often too centralized and over-dimensioned, took precedence over adjusting organizational structures, changes in job structures and modernization of industrial relations. Today, this delay in implementing changes seems to threaten the current strategies to escape from the crisis.

An awareness of fashionable trends

One might think that this explains why, in the 1980s, French companies attempted *en masse* to introduce new methods of change management. Companies certainly had a better press from public opinion as policies were introduced. They came thick and fast: 'Qualité Totale' (TQM), Cercles de Progrès' (quality circles), 'Management Participatif' (participative management), 'Audits Culturels' (cultural audits), 'l'Ethique d'Entreprise' (Corporate ethics). In the past few years, France has been one of the European countries to have implemented these new methods in industry and, in particular, in the services sector and state services most strongly. Nevertheless, the results are full of nuances. We can observe that a great number of experiments failed, especially those that took place in large nationalized companies. In many SMEs, in contrast, it seems that such experiments have played a key role in neutralizing union action and developing individual motivation.

In recent years France went through other social innovations aimed at remedying the crisis in work systems. For example, in the 1970s, 'New Forms of Organization', inspired by the Swedish 'Industrial Democracy', were put forward by some managers. But they suffered from impermanency, even if, as New Forms of Work Organization, they were heavily publicized as panaceas for improving industrial performance.

HRM to the fore

We need to understand the recent vogue of the technologies developed in human resources management (HRM) in France. Are these 'invisible technologies' an attempt at easing social relationships or improving productivity?

The development of HRM in French management cannot be denied. It can be illustrated either by the increase of training courses dedicated to this subject since the beginning of the 1980s or by the importance of this function today in corporate technostructure.

In only one decade – the 1980s – the gross salary of personnel managers was multiplied by three in France. This sector is, without doubt, still fragile and varies according to the fluctuations of economic climate (the crisis in 1990 brought about the decline in this sector). The HRM function, as in other countries, still has problems of positioning. Should it be centralized and constitute a department of specialists or should it be applied to more specific problems? Whatever its precise orientation, the strategic trend throughout is towards using its services to better engineer a 'global competitiveness', i.e. a competitiveness which would attempt at combining economic efficiency and social achievement, the winning of market shares and the development (in numbers as well as quality) of jobs.

References

1 Weber, M., *L'Ethique protestante et l'esprit du capitalisme*, 1st edn, 1904–1905.
2 Le Bras, H. and Todd, E., *L'invention de la France*, Editions Puriel Paris, p. 72.
3 Gervais, M., Servolin, Cl. and Weil, J., *Une France sans paysans*, Le Seuil, Paris, 1965.
4 Jeanneney, J.-M., 'L'heritage et le poids du passé', in *Observations et diagnostics économiques*, Paris, Lettre de l'OFCE, No. 68, October 1989.
5 Jeanneney, J.-M., *L'invention de l'Europe*, Le Seuil, Paris, 1990, p. 537.
6 DATAR and le Commissariat Général du Plan.
7 Reynaud, J.-D., *Les syndicats en France*, Volums 1, Le Seuil, Paris, 1975, p. 68.
8 Reberioux, M., *La république radicale*, Le Seuil, Paris, 1975, p. 75.
9 Sellier, F., *La confrontation sociale en France, 1936–1981*, PUF, Paris, 1984, p. 238.
10 Dalle, F. and Bounine, J., *L'Education en entreprise. Coutre le chômage des jeunes*, Editions Odile Jacob, Paris, 1993, p. 282.
11 Riboud, A., *Modernisation, mode d'emploi*, Christian Bourgois Editions, Paris, 1987, p. 214. Sudreau Report – La réforme de l'entreprise; Stoleru Report – Les conditions de travail; Wisner Report – Le travail posté; Giraudet Report – Les bas salaires. (Reports produced between 1975 and 1977.)
12 'Travail et emploi', *Dossier emploi*, No. 52, February 1992, 109.
13 Bibes, G. and Mouriaux, R., *Les syndicats européens à l'épreuve*, Presses de la Fondation Nationale des Sciences Politiques, Paris, 1990: Institut de Recherches Economiques et Sociales (IRES), *Syndicalismes. Dynamique des relations professionnelles*, Dunod, Paris, 1992, p. 461.
14 Bunel, F. and Saglio, J., *L'action patronale*, PUF, Paris, 1979, p. 97.

15 Dufour, Ch., *Les Syndicalismes. Dynamique des relations professionnelles*, Dunod, Paris, 1992, p. 461.

16 Weber, H., 'Le parti des patrons. Le CNPF (1946–1986)', and Bauer, M., 'Pas de sociologie de l'entreprise sans sociologie de ses dirigeants', in Sainsaulieu, R. (ed.), *L'entreprise une affaire de société*, Presses de la Foundation Nationale des Sciences Politiques, Paris, 1990, pp. 148–174.

17 Bauer, M. and Bertin-Mourot, B., *Les 200 en France et en Allemagne. Deux modèles contrastés de détection–sélection–formation de dirigeants de grandes entreprises*, CNRS, Paris. A synthesis of this research can be found in *La Revue de l'IRES*, No. 10, Autumn, 1992, 31–70.

18 Boltanski, L., *Les cadres. La formation d'un groupe social*, Editions de Minuit, Paris, 1982, p. 523.

19 Taddei, D. and Coriat, B., *Made in France. L'industrie française dans la compétition mondiale*, Le Livre de Poche, Paris, 1993, p. 471.

20 Crozier, M., *Le phénomène bureaucratique*, Editions du Seuil, Paris, 1963, p. 382.

21 d'Iribarne, P., La logique de l'honneur: Gestion des entreprises et traditions nationales, Editions du Seuil, Paris, 1989.

5 Managing people in Central Europe

Velimir Srica

Introduction

Intensity of change has become the main feature of the world in which we live. The countries of Central and Eastern Europe are probably experiencing this fact of life to a much greater extent than any other part of the world.

The collapse of the hegemony system operated by the former Soviet Union has left them not only free to exploit opportunities but also vitally exposed to the threat of not being able to cope with change. To survive, they must learn what some call the new methods and others 'the new tricks' of modern management, modern entrepreneurship, modern capitalism, and the modern market economy. Their old bottles cannot hold the new wine, either.

After the fall of the old socialist regimes there is, fortunately, a new spirit of entrepreneurship and an explosion of change taking place in the emergent market economies of Eastern and Central Europe. The safe economic and social zoo, in which the market forces were kept behind the bars of strict government control and most individuals were living a life of protected animals in an ideological cage, is now changing. As everything had been taken care of for them from cradle to grave by 'society', the individuals were not accustomed to initiatives. But the change did take place. The safe, although unpleasant, cages have been replaced by the dangerous marketplace-jungle where only the fittest survives. Such crudeness of language is not unjustified by the facts of the situation. There are certainly more chances for success there, but there are also major risks and uncertainties.

The management environment of former socialist countries of Central Europe is nowadays characterized by the growing lack of social security, a tentative acceptance of democracy, a fear of mass unemployment and an emerging need to improvise in order to survive. As such, it may be well suited for new businesses and new approaches to managing people in certain sectors of industry and commerce, but not in others.

The pre-revolutionary business environment in Central European 'socialist' countries could be described by the following characteristics:

1 The majority of businesses and assets were nationalized (except for some small-scale private industry and small farms).
2 Enterprises were state owned and, in most cases, responsible to either central government or to the local authorities.
3 Enterprises were 'unincorporated' (without share capital).
4 Even though enjoying some autonomy, business enterprises behaved as an extension of the civil service.
5 The system of subsidies was heavily distorting business performance (subsidized raw material costs, energy input costs, unrealistic interest rates and consumer price subsidies).
6 Top management positions were usually held by party members or officials regardless of their skills and performance.
7 Enterprises were managed in such a way that many key decisions were imposed on them by state and/or local government bodies.
8 Instead of bankruptcy the troubled enterprises were absorbed within the more successful ones, according to the political dictate. Typically, there were no laws on bankruptcy.
9 Most trade with the West was conducted through monopolistic national foreign trade organizations.
10 Most trade with the Comecon countries was based on either negotiated or imposed production quotas. The transferable currency unit used had no objective value.
11 Labour costs were kept very low and most enterprises were overstaffed.
12 Management's achievements were, in principle, not measured by financial performance of enterprises.
13 The planning and accounting functions were organized in such a way to provide central statistics with data on plan fulfilment and to ensure that taxes were properly administered and collected.
14 Production-based decision-making processes in enterprises more often than not ignored the commercial and marketing effects of the decisions.
15 Relatively strong basic research was mostly academic, and there were very few commercial applications of domestic science.
16 Quality-awareness in enterprises was low because the demand for goods and services usually exceeded supply. Rationing of many classes of consumer goods was the norm.
17 Entrepreneurship, management and business administration were not taught in schools, and economic education at all levels was heavily ideologized.
18 Banks and other financial institutions were controlled by government, and often their decisions were based on political and not economic arguments.
19 So far as workers' rights were concerned, social issues often prevailed

over professional ones, causing a lack of motivation and discipline as well as an overprotectionism.

20 Rigid, autocratic but often-changing enterprise legislation produced an irrational bureaucratic syndrome. People accepted and passively followed the letter of the law. Safety came first whatever the logic.

These features have left a significant impact on the present situation and still influence to great extent the environment in which managers in Central Europe live and act.

Historical background

Austria-Hungary was a dual monarchy dominating the area of Central and Eastern Europe for several centuries. In 1918, after the First World War it was divided among Austria, Czechoslovakia, Hungary, Slovenia, Croatia, Bosnia and Herzegovina and parts of land were lost to Italy and Poland. It used to be a large and powerful state with a population of over 50 million people. Its capitals, Vienna and Budapest, two of the world's great cities, were known for trade and culture. The economy of Austria-Hungary was based on farms, factories, mineral deposits and important land routes, including the Danube, a great river highway of Europe.

As a multinational (a dozen major nations), multiconfessional (Catholics, Protestants, Orthodox, Muslims, Jewish) and multicultural country, the Austro-Hungarian empire had both its government and the economy characterized by a high degree of independence and distribution of authorities. In political terms it was a combination of union of independent states and confederacy with well-defined laws and rather efficient bureaucracies. In economic terms it was a successful, unevenly-developed but patently European marketplace, a booming capitalist state with a strong cultural identity. Its educational system was among the best in the world, especially as far as the multilingual and multicultural aspects were concerned. Even though 45 years of post-war socialist-communist history have led the empire's component countries down different paths, the centuries of common Austro-Hungarian experience are still the strong, if latent, common denominator.

In principle, Central Europe consists of six countries (the Czech Republic, Slovakia, Hungary, Austria, Croatia and Slovenia). Due to the recent separation of Czechoslovakia into two states as well as to the lack of available data, we will concentrate more on Austria, Hungary, Croatia and Slovenia. Some basic facts about the area (1989 and 1990 data) are given in Table 5.1.

Austria is a typical economy of Western Europe and, except for the geographical proximity and cultural similarities, it has a little to do with other

Table 5.1

Country	Population (millions)	Growth (%)	Area (000 km²)	GNP per capita (US$)
Austria	7.6	0.15	83.85	16 600
Croatia	4.8	0.31	56.54	3.200
Czechoslovakia	15.7	1.90	127.90	2.250
Hungary	10.6	0.17	93.03	2 900
Slovenia	1.9	0.22	20.25	4.700

countries in the region. The location of Austria on the German border and its guarded language and culture have stamped it quite identifiably since the Thirty Years' War (1618–1648) as belonging to the German sphere of influence. From the management point of view Croatia, Hungary and Slovenia seem to be somewhat similar cases of so-called 'emerging market economies'. These three countries were at the forefront of development and change within the former socialist world of Central and Eastern Europe. Even though ideologically close to the Communist economies under the former Soviet Union umbrella, Croatia and Slovenia (as the most developed parts of former Yugoslavia) belonged to the so-called 'non-allied world' and were, in principle, semi-market economies. On the other hand, Hungary was the first to depart from the rigid Soviet model and already within the old system was practising various economic reforms.

The dominant religion in the area is Catholicism. Unlike some other religions, the Catholics placed a relatively low emphasis on wealth acquisition. Getting rich and prosperous was not a highly valued goal in their culture, possibly due to papal pronouncements on usury from the eleventh century onwards. Such an attitude is still reflected in the prevailing managerial culture of Central Europe, even though now to a much smaller extent.

Another important facet of the local managerial (and overall) culture is rising nationalism. After the fall of Communism there is an ever-growing need to re-evaluate national history, to build an awareness of national heritage, to develop a new identity based on self-esteem and feeling of national reunion. Even though it sometimes goes too far into autarky, isolation and economic protectionism, the growing nationalism in Central Europe is mainly defensive. In addition, such an attitude is not deeply rooted in the culture and history of the area partly because of the permissiveness of the Hapsburgs. Its impact may diminish in time.

In 1978 in Venice a regional association of the countries belonging to Central Europe was founded. It consists of five Austrian, two Hungarian, four Italian provinces, Croatia, Slovenia and the German 'Free state'

Bavaria. For more than 10 years it has served as a bridge between the developed countries of Western and Central Europe and the reformist parts of the former Yugoslavia and Hungary. The name of the association, 'Alps-Adriatic Working Community', reflects its ambition of promoting cooperation in the areas of economy, tourism, transportation, health, ecology, science, education, culture and sport. Numerous activities have promoted many common interests and opened different processes. For example, they increased commercial cooperation and mobility of human resources, initiated exchange of students and scholars, supported mutual research and technology-transfer projects, and, above all, revitalized the common spirit of Central Europe.

Yugoslavia used to be a country composed of different nations, each possessing its own culture, language, religion, traditional links and aspirations and a well-defined territory. It was one of the products of the Versailles Treaty in 1918. Before that, these nations lived their separate lives for almost a thousand years – Croatia and Slovenia as parts of the Austro-Hungarian Empire and Serbia, Bosnia and others ruled by the Turkish Empire for five centuries. Therefore, except for the 1918–1991 period, Yugoslavia (a land of southern Slavs) never existed throughout the history of these nations.

Needless to say, the destruction of Austria-Hungary in the First World War put them together in a rather artificial way. The new country was first ruled by the Serbian dynasty Karageorgevic, and later by Tito's Communists and the Army. Under both regimes a significant portion of income of more developed Croatia and Slovenia was redistributed to the under-developed republics.

After the Second World War all private enterprises in Yugoslavia were nationalized, and even the private farms were restricted to only five hectares of land. In the early 1950s the state-directed economy was gradually replaced by a combination of planned and market economy. A new concept, 'self-management' was introduced in all enterprises with more than five employees. This meant that formally the workers held a dominant position in decision-making processes (in practice, the political leaders kept controlling, or at least directing the decision-making process, but 'behind the scenes'). A unique model of social ownership of the means of production was introduced and the political as well as industrial culture were both negative, in some cases even hostile, towards managers and entrepreneurs.

During the next twenty years the self-management model did try to create conditions for reforming the national economy, with varying success. Some progress was made in terms of social development, as, for example, equal opportunities for housing, health care, education, etc. However, the latent conflict between the state and self-management in the early 1970s gradually led to an open crisis. Government spending was exceeding the capacity of the economy to produce the required wealth. Instead of initiating democratic changes and accelerating technological development, Yugoslavia started to increase its external debt and was entangled in endless discussions about how to improve the self-management system without really changing it. As the economy of the country started to decline, the unsolved political problems tended to get larger and more disturbing. The suppressed nationalisms started to grow, triggered by an aggressive campaign in Serbia in the late 1980s.

In 1989 the newly formed Federal government, headed by Ante Markovic, initiated a series of market-oriented reforms. These were directed towards: (1) establishment of an integral market (goods, services, capital, labour); (2) introduction of international standards and liberalization of foreign trade; and (3) development of a modern legal environment in both economy and society. Even though the initial results were encouraging, the political tensions grew faster. It was too late for Yugoslavia to survive.

After the demise of Communism in Europe in 1990, in the first free elections, non-Communist parties won in four (out of six) federal units and the disintegration process was on its way. The exceptions were the largest (Serbia) and the smallest republic (Montenegro). They still have in power the old, basically Communist regimes, recently disguised as 'socialist parties'. Their aggressive strategy, first of 'preserving Yugoslavia' and later of 'creating one country for all the Serbs', as well as the accumulated economic and political discrepancies, were the sources of the wars in Slovenia (summer 1991), Croatia (1991–1992) and Bosnia and Herzegovina (1992+).

During the Communist period the legal system in all countries of Eastern/Central Europe was radically changed. The same happened to Yugoslavia. However, the first ideological wave that was based on the Soviet model lasted for only five years. After breaking with the USSR in 1948, Yugoslavia gradually developed a new ideological construction, a unique self-management system which was based on social ownership, partial openness to the legal standards and norms of Western Europe, and bureaucratic litigiousness. This did, in fact, manifest itself as an organizational dysfunction, with executives made powerless by the array of laws, norms and regulations with which they were confronted. The legal systems of Croatia and Slovenia are now undergoing transformation from the previous social-ownership and self-management socialism to a modern European private-property capitalism. Both countries have been admitted to the United Nations and were recognized as independent states in January 1992.

Present situation

Let us now focus on the present and look at several 'comparative advantages' that describe the management and business arena in which modern post-socialist managers in Central Europe perform.

1 *Fresh motivation*. The changing environment of Central Europe is an interesting arena for new enterprises, ideas and innovations. Unlike other 'stable' markets and societies in Europe, these countries provide various motivating challenges as well as strong incentives.

2 *Willingness to learn*. The emerging market economies are trying to shake off the obstructive old habits. Most white-collar employees are ready to compete and learn the ways of the developed world. The availability of information, know-how and some model-experiences of the 'newly industrialized' countries (e.g. in South-east Asia) provide a flow of concepts to be tested and applied in Central and Eastern Europe.

3 *Talent for improvisation*. Many Central Europeans have shown in the last decades a high ability to improvise and thus accommodate for the continuing lack of infrastructure, inadequate organization and deficiencies in legal or institutional arrangements for business initiatives.

4 *Large potential markets*. The emerging market economies of Central Europe are still short in housing, construction, consumer goods and services, thus creating a large and growing domestic market for all kinds of initiatives and new businesses. In the period before the Second World War several of them were larger than West European neighbours.

5 *Educational system*. In general, well-educated Central Europeans can easily compete with anyone. Although there were no management schools until recently, good professional programmes, particularly in technology and the natural sciences, provide a number of competent experts in various fields, important for modern technological development. The underlying commercial traditions are German.

6 *Self-financing*. The ratio of savings to earnings was very high in the economies of Central Europe, due to the lack of goods and services. Therefore, in principle, there is an availability of initial private capital for starting new small businesses. These are prudent people.

7 *Competitive wages*. The price of labour in Central Europe is usually only a fraction of the same cost in developed economies. This is particularly true for certain important professions (e.g. engineers, medical doctors or scientists). The less convertible the currency, the more marked is this advantage.

8 *Emerging entrepreneurs*. The dynamic environment of Central Europe has already resulted in some good examples of successful entrepreneurs to be studied and replicated by others.

9 *Emigrant links*. The United States and Western Europe has accepted several waves of emigrants from the emerging market economies of Central Europe. Among them there are well-established businessmen, scholars, educators or scientists who could serve as a bridge connecting new business initiatives with the developed world markets.

10 *Suppressed creativity*. There are many suppressed talents throughout the

countries of Central Europe. Having been relatively isolated from the mainstream of world development in different areas, these individuals are eager to enter the global competition and express their creativity to the maximum.

11 *Favourable environment.* Unlike during the period of the cold war, the countries of Central Europe are surrounded by the friendly, cooperative spirit of the European Union. Such an environment could easily lead to new developments in the former socialist world.

Since the methods of business management in a market economy differ from those in (semi-)planned economies, we should expect that the residue of organizational and management culture which was appropriate for the old system must pose serious problems for the managers in the emerging market economies, willing to integrate into the world marketplace. A highly pertinent research study recently carried out by the World Economic Forum and the IMD concentrated on several critical development management issues, such as:

- The overall role of the manager – what is a manager and what should he or she do? What are the preferable characteristics and traits of modern managers? What is the source of their authority? What is the self-perception of managers?
- The role of managers in formulating goals and visions – how the visions and goals are determined. What is the time horizon? What are perceived as the main goals and targets? What strategies are selected and how?
- Managers' perception of their environment – criteria for success; expected values, attitudes and ways of thinking; social patterns and relations to others.
- Values and norms governing organizational behaviour – social issues, expected behaviour, conflict resolution; group values; responsibilities and decision-making practices; relationship with the boss.

The main hypothesis and findings are summarized in Table 5.2. The study showed that most managers from Central and Eastern Europe share their traditional values to a much greater extent. There was also a strong correlation with age, education and their position in the organization. The younger, better-educated and less responsible managers tend to show more appreciation for modern management thinking. The findings have also revealed significant differences which could be attributed to the semi-market economies in Croatia and Slovenia, as opposed to Hungary. The attitudes, norms and values of Croatian and Slovenian managers were, in principle, shifted more to the right, when compared with the Hungarian managers.

As in other former socialist countries, management approaches have been

Table 5.2

Issues	Traditional management thinking	Modern management thinking
1 What is a manager?		
Description	Policeman, officer, politician, thief	Leader, friend, coach, conductor
Important traits	Experience, loyalty, decisiveness, ruthlessness	Morality, vision, leadership, will to cooperate
Self-perception	Politicized, socially isolated	Avoids politics, present in public
Source of authority	Position, rank power	Competence, charisma
Selection	Experience, years of work, political	Education, references, professional.
2 Setting the goals		
General approach	Ideological	Pragmatic
Main target	Production quantity	Marketing, quality
Time frame	Short-term	Long-term
Main goals	Survival, stability	Success, growth
Strategy	Risk adverse	Risk taking
3 Perception of the environment		
Thinking scope	Local, autarkic	Global, cosmopolitan
Criteria of success	National	International
Attitude	Conservatism	Innovation
Relation to others	Collaboration	Competition
Expected values	Social justice, equality	Success, fair-play
Social pattern	Collectivism	Individualism
4 Organizational values and norms		
Social issues	Egalitarianism	Exclusivity
Expected behaviour	Commitment	Professionalism
Conflict resolution	Loyalty, punishment	Adaptation, cooperation
Relationship	Obedience	Initiative
With the boss	Guardianship	Self-dependence
Group values	uniformity, conformity, integration	Differentiation, creativity, self-esteem
Responsibility	Delegated	Shared
Decision making	Authoritative	Participative

heavily influenced by quantitative thinking instead of relevant concepts of how to manage and motivate people. Management by reports and management by political expectations are to be replaced by management by results in the new scenario. Many old-style managers will be strongly averse to change.

Introducing modern management

If you were to ask any representative of business, government or academic community in Croatia, Hungary or Slovenia about the priorities of economic development, it is certain that a need to develop modern management and entrepreneurship would be among the first items on the list. To promote modern management and entrepreneurship in Central and Eastern Europe means at least two things:

- To create a favourable macro-economic environment
- To overcome attitudinal barriers.

As far as the macroeconomic issues are concerned, there have been initial successes in stabilizing inflation rates, getting federal budgets under control, privatizing the economy and establishing a legal system of property rights as well as trying to establish a convertible currency. By eliminating the legal barriers to modern market economy, as Harvard Professor Jeffrey Sachs would suggest, the right macroeconomic environment should stimulate and support the economic development.

There are four key government policies which are currently still necessary prerequisites for modern management and entrepreneurial development in Poland, Czechia, Slovenia and Hungary:

1 The provision of sound macroeconomic, legal, financial and fiscal environment for the business community.
2 The development of an appropriate infrastructure to provide training, finance, technology transfer and other business services to enterprises.
3 The establishment of suitable conditions to ensure international trade, investment and cooperation.
4 The application of all the necessary international standards concerning economic and business environment.

Further progress needs to be made in all four dimensions.

Perceptions vary on how successful government policies and reforms are in the various countries analysed above. In Hungary most people already experience the favourable changes and consider the government policies rather successful. Slovenian managers are a little less enthusiastic, while Croatian managers think that the economic reforms have not as yet been implemented or have failed. The parallel or black economy (unreported and tax-avoiding economic activities) is an important feature of Central Europe. The survey findings show that in three countries analysed (Croatia, Hungary and Slovenia), managers consider these activities very important. On a scale from 0 = low to 100 = high importance, the assessment of managers was between 52 in Croatia and 69 in Hungary.

The survey supports the belief that substantial increased contact with foreign cultures and nations is of interest to the domestic population of these countries. Foreigners are most welcome and accepted in Croatia, only a little less in Slovenia and Hungary. As far as the regulations dealing with joint ventures and international trade are concerned, the most satisfied are Hungarian and the least satisfied are Croatian managers. Joint ventures are a major source of development not only for large but also for small and medium sized companies. 'Rolitron', from Hungary, is an example of such a company. In 1991 it was a producer of computer hardware and software with 250 employees and a turnover of US$10 million per year when it merged with B. Brown AG, a multinational German company with annual sales of DM 2 billion, operating in 40 countries around the world. After the merger an autonomous research and development centre was created, launching several programmes to develop new devices in the medical field. Consequently, the firm acquired 30 per cent of the Hungarian network of dialysis stations with 260 employees.

One of the transitional problems of the emerging market economies is the lack of decision-making authority. In many cases it is not clear with whom to negotiate, who has power to make economic decisions and who has responsibility for their implementation. Among many examples there is a case of a large manufacturer of cement in Croatia. After many months of negotiations several potential foreign partners decided to quit. Each time they found they would have to negotiate with different partners. On one occasion it was a senior government official from Zagreb, then it was one of the company directors, another time it was a head of the local community, etc. Such problems are expected to be gradually solved by faster privatization and by diminishing government control of enterprises. It is also the notion that companies are managed within a social ownership framework – rather than purely economically run – that poses a major problem.

Another typical managerial problem is the changing size and scope of the activity of organizations, which is not an outcome of market forces but rather has political or legislative origin. Cromont, the parent of Chepromont, a Croatian firm, was founded in 1950 as a merger between two enterprises. The first was dealing with equipment and machine repair and the second with vehicle servicing and development of tools. The rapid growth of the new firm during the 1950s and 1960s is closely associated with the period of the industrialization of Croatia. The domestic market has exhibited continuously growing demand for development and assembly of chemical plants, energy equipment and other construction for almost 30 years. In 1957 Cromont entered the world market as a subcontractor of an Austrian firm, successfully completing the construction of a power plant in Lebanon. By the end of the 1980s the changing political situation as well as new legislation was used to initiate disintegration. One of the most vital parts of the old firm, the team specialized for building chemical and other process plants, was from 1989 organized as a new enterprise, Chepromont, and thus separated from the parent firm.

Among other 'macroeconomic' problems that are often stressed by managers in Central Europe one might emphasize the following:

1 The government has assumed a leading role in the economy, state control and ownership of business enterprises, affecting competition and dominating or distorting the market.
2 Members of state and local governments are not competent to deal with the challenges of transition, or the government is not transparent (does not communicate its intentions to citizens).
3 Bribing and corruption still have a serious impact on all public affairs.
4 There is much to be done in regulating bankruptcy, private ownership, corporate accounts and property rights.
5 The development of fair fiscal policies and modern tax systems is not yet completed.
6 Stock markets, insurance institutions and local banks are not as yet adequately developed; laws and regulations of financial institutions are incomplete or lacking.
7 Infrastructure (power, distribution systems, transport, communication) is still inadequate to support effective business development.
8 Intellectual property needs better protection, there is a significant brain drain, R&D is still not geared towards innovation and technological dependence is growing.

The attitudinal barriers stem, on the one hand, from a lack of creative, innovative and risk-taking personalities, and, on the other, from a reactive and cautious culture, unready to accept and promote competitive, risk-oriented and innovation-oriented behaviour. As an example, let us take Rade Koncar, a large manufacturer of electrical and electronic products, again based in Croatia. In 1990, after the new market-oriented philosophy had been introduced, the first action to be taken by the new management was to dismiss the majority of about 2000 engineers and technicians, employed in the centrally organized Research/Development Department, a counterproductive move in terms of the company's longer-term strategic development.

Perceptions also vary on how successfully the individuals, managers or workers in the countries analysed cope with the cultural and attitudinal side of reforms. In Hungary and Slovenia slightly more people believe that entrepreneurship and risk taking pay off than in Croatia. In all countries of Central Europe there is much individual initiative, but the motivation to work differs. Interestingly enough, people in the majority seem now not to be much more motivated to work. The degree of motivation is associated with ownership. As an example, in 1990 in Hungary some 20 000 new companies were formed. But four-fifths of the new enterprises were not private so much as privatized state enterprises. Their market success was less than was the case with thousands of truly private initiatives that were expanding in 1982 as the outcome of early economic liberalization in that country.

The first problem of many firms is privatization or transformation of the former social ownership. For example, Kandit, a food-producing company from Croatia had its value estimated at US $5 350 000. The majority of the stock was purchased by the managers of the firm as well as by the employees. The new owners, already employed by the firm, were able to purchase shares at 20–40 per cent discount. The assembly of shareholders (mainly employees) selected a board of directors (five members) and appointed the former director as the General manager. Such an arrangement (the employees are principal owners) derives from the well-advanced, self-management culture in Croatian business enterprises, providing a high degree of worker participation in decision making. It, hopefully, will create a secure basis for the firm's future economic success.

One of the crucial problems is the changing economic and political geography in the region. New strategies and business orientations are inescapable. For example, after the disintegration of the former Yugoslavia, Montaza, the large Slovenian industrial plant, equipment and construction firm, had lost most of its traditional market (one-third of it was in Bosnia and Herzegovina) and had to change its overall strategy. The emphasis was shifted towards the Near and the Far East as well as Africa. Also some partnerships and joint ventures have been initiated with several traditional partners from Western Europe (Germany, the Netherlands, Austria). The major competitors on the world market are firms from Central and Eastern Europe (Poland, Hungary) as well as the growing companies from South and East Asia (South Korea, China, the Philippines). Typical problems in obtaining large contracts, including credit lines for the buyer, use of local workers, total service to the customer (plant, equipment, technology, knowhow, maintenance), have been transformed by the lack of political certainty.

Surveys and analyses indicated that most of the private initiative enterprises that have emerged is the past couple of years provide services and few have been engaged in industrial activities. But there is tough competition. For instance, Caster, one of the most successful computer companies in the Czech Republic, was on a brink of collapse in 1991. After a rapid growth in personal computer sales Caster got into trouble when a large state-owned customer could not pay its debt – a not-untypical occurrence. With no bankruptcy law, firms like Caster had no legal protection against secondary insolvency.

As far as the attitudinal barriers are concerned, managers in Central Europe tend to identify the following issues:

1 Employees do not participate enough in decision making (even in view of the legacy of statutory systems for this) and do not show initiative.
2 There is still a high level of employee turnover and absenteeism, especially in state enterprises. Employees do not identify with hard work.
3 The relationship between managers and employees tends to deteriorate over time.
4 There is too much short-term thinking and a situational approach. People tend not to plan their activities in the long run.
5 The concept of quality is heavily neglected and therefore the price/quality ratio of domestic products and services is low when compared with international competitors.
6 Managers and corporations do not always behave in a responsible manner, especially as far as ecological issues and the utilization of scarce resources are concerned. The reward–punishment system has not been conducive to efforts in this area.

One of the issues that should be explored further is the so-called 'egalitarian attitude' which is still prevailing in all the former non-market or semi-market economies of Central Europe. As opposed to the Western concept of equal opportunity, the 'egalitarian syndrome', implanted in minds of most people in emerging market economies, is based on the following:

• Egalitarian distribution – a belief that personal income should never exceed certain limits, irrespective of individual contribution, outcome or performance. This belief appears to be most strongly held in Poland among members of the Solidarnosc (Solidarity) trade union.
• Redistributional ethics – a moral obligation on an individual to share his or her property with others.
• Anti-intellectualism – a glorification of physical effort and underestimation of intellectual work or knowledge. The former Soviet Union contributed to this through the creed of Stakhanovism (reorganizing work processes to increase production).
• Anti-innovation – a negative attitude towards individual creativity, innovation and entrepreneurship.

Table 5.3

Country	Manufacturing worker	Middle manager	Chief executive officer (CEO)
	(average 1991 per hour compensation in US $)		
Austria	17.50	26.00	
Croatia	1.56	3.33	6.18
Czechoslovakia	0.80	1.00	4.70
Hungary	0.88	5.00	12.00
Poland	0.92	4.50	7.00
Slovenia	2.04	3.94	6.57

Even though such concepts are not supported by any official ideology of 'post-socialism' in Central Europe, some sociological studies indicate that many facets of the egalitarian syndrome still strongly influence the behaviour of managers and workers in these countries.

The labour market

One of the areas in which the traditional efforts on the road from pre-market to market economies seem to be rather difficult is the labour market. Many elements of such markets existed in the old Czechoslovakia, Croatia and Slovenia. At the very least, since the borders were relatively open, some people with higher skills or knowledge could move abroad and thus participate in a continuing brain drain (Table 5.3).

It is worth noting that the laws governing labour markets in Hungary, Slovenia and Croatia favour employers and give substantial rights to management. The unions have a rather small impact on the state of affairs. Their legal power and their real influence could both be described as limited. What seems to be happening can be termed the 'pendulum effect'!

The pendulum of official ideology previously used to be 'too much to the left' (workers' rights and social issues were always more important than business efficiency). The current reaction to this is 'too much to the right' (workers' rights and social issues seem to be pushed to the margin of political interest) in favour of greater economic efficiency. It will take some time before 'the pendulum rests in the middle', as a result of a more balanced approach. However, due to the still-unstable political situation, in most cases the pressure from the unions will be for a maintenance of pay increases. Poland's strikes and political unrest in 1992/1993 are indicative of this pressure. As an outcome, there is a growing antagonism between the government (still representing the major employer) and the unions over the exact level of productivity gain (if any) that is conceded for the pay rises.

As far as unemployment, social security, pensions, health insurance, safety and similar issues are concerned, the socialist/Communist societies of Central Europe have developed elaborate systems, in theory described as 'fair and free' and in practice implemented as 'free and low quality'. Now such systems are undergoing deep change since they are both inappropriate and uneconomic.

In Slovenia and Croatia, for example, labour relations are regulated by so-called collective agreements. They are concluded and signed at the level of the state and at the level of each branch of industry. Such agreements describe the rights and obligations of all employees and their wages/salaries, etc. Individual employment is regulated by a temporary service contract, i.e. an employment contract. There are special managerial contracts which describe the rights and duties of managers as well as the appropriate compensations for their work.

Education of managers has been recognized as one of the critical issues in all emerging market economies. Between 75 and 85 per cent from a sample of middle and top managers from Croatia, Slovenia, the former Czechoslovakia and Hungary strongly agree with the statement that there is a lack of competent managers in each of these countries, due predominantly to educational shortcomings.

Let us illustrate human resources management in a successful firm in Central Europe by taking cases as examples. Case 1 is a construction firm in Slovenia. It is functionally organized and there are basically five types of departments: Marketing, Production, Finance, Human Resources, Engineering. The general manager is responsible for the overall business strategy and for coordination in planning the activities in different departments. The department managers develop their action plans and are responsible for implementation of the company strategy. The working sites are relatively independent in their operational decision making but must follow the general strategy and the principles of the firm. Working sites are organized in matrix form with task forces responsible for local contracts. However, the central Finance, Marketing and Production departments are responsible for efficiency control, mainly expressed in financial terms.

There are 1350 people employed in the firm, of which 10 per cent are college graduates (mostly engineers), and 60 per cent are highly skilled workers or technicians. The activity of the human resources department is directed towards the following four tasks:

- Recruitment and selection
- Motivation and stimulation

- Education and training
- Reward and pay system

Employee selection is based on tests and interviews. In most cases the decisions to hire a person are made by managers. However, the general manager is responsible for hiring the managers within departments. Special attention is paid to selection and hiring of managers, and the selection process is based on an analysis of an applicant's intellectual abilities, communication skills, managerial skills, developed relationships with subordinates and personality. These are evaluated through a series of tests and interviews. Motivation and stimulation of employees are based on strategic plans and basically consist of a set of punishment/reward schemes.

Due to the growing international orientation of the firm, as far as education and training are concerned, special attention is paid to learning foreign languages. Similarly, employees are sent on short professional courses, and, in some cases in-house training and retraining is organized. Certain jobs are specially rewarded with respect to time-keeping and high quality standards. Loyalty to the firm, expressed in years of service, is also financially rewarded. Distinguished workers receive diplomas, medals and extra vacations.

The late 1980s and the early 1990s have seen a growing number of new programmes and institutions providing continuous executive education and business administration courses as well as different professional courses for managers. Most of these institutions and programmes have been initiated and developed with help and support from the West. In Croatia there are presently three graduate business administration programmes/schools. In Slovenia there is a distinguished international centre for executive development and several other programmes. In Hungary there are half a dozen institutions/programmes for educating managers, most of them in Budapest. Similarly, Poland and Czechoslovakia have made significant progress in establishing new business schools.

For many firms radical changes in a company's functioning are considered to be the necessary prerequisites for entering the global market. Hence, the extent to which such firms use the courses provided for senior management training. This construction firm has, in fact, put all its top managers through appropriate courses in the last 3 years.

Case 2 concerns Badel, the leading manufacturer of beverages and spirits in Croatia. After privatization, its new management decided to get rid of the old organizational culture and the former self-management approach (and associated attitudes) and to improve the image of the firm. As critical factors for success they pointed out the following:

- The need to develop a modern management information system
- The requirement to improve awareness of the changes in technology

- The need to better educate the managers
- The lack of financial resources
- The lack of information about competitors

In order to improve the organizational culture and image of the firm, Badel hired an international consultant. As a first step a videocassette describing the firm, its references and its major strengths had been prepared as promotional material. The firm has since become a sponsor of a successful handball team from Zagreb who is expected to participate in international competition.

The management has recently decided to use a matrix rather than a purely functional organization structure throughout the firm whenever possible, to design and organize all the activities as projects with project leaders and independent financial budgets, to promote consensus as the decision-making philosophy and to develop a close relationship with a Croatian business school (courses, consulting, projects, etc.). Special attention is paid to development of negotiating skills of all the managers dealing with international markets.

There is a growing network of activities and efforts to integrate the emerging market economies of Central Europe in the developed world. As an example, in order to promote and improve cooperation within the area as well as with the West, Slovenia, Croatia and Hungary have initiated the establishment of an association of management schools from Central and Eastern Europe. CEEMAN was founded in 1993 and its first seat is in Ljubljana, Slovenia.

Conclusions

The Vyshegrad countries – Poland, Hungary, Czechia and Slovakia – are so-called because of their agreement at the start of the 1990s (made at Vyshegrad) to consider their economic and political interests collectively, as well as individually, in framing trade policies. They have all now been accepted as associate members of the European Union and have high hopes of negotiating full entry by the turn of the millennium. They also have high hopes – and not unreasonable expectations – of restoring themselves and the Vyshegrad region to the prosperity enjoyed before the Second World War. At that time, Poland and Czechoslovakia in particular were two of Europe's leading economies. In spite of the debilitating effects of civil war in the former Yugoslavia, Slovenia and Croatia have similar potential aspirations.

To realize the hoped-for progress much needs to be done, as this chapter suggests. There is a need for macropolitical stabilization around the twin desiderata of democracy and the rule of law. The first is problematic, because those accustomed to totalitarianism see political debate more as a sign of a state's weakness than of its strength. The second is problematic, given the entrenched position of Central European Mafiosi and the black market. There is need for macroeconomic advance. This concerns currency stability, anti-inflation policies and high spending on human capital investment programmes such as management education.

Such patterns of change are mandatory. Yet they are exceptionally difficult to mastermind because:

1 Central European countries are typically heavily indebted and need to use many of their resources (from exports) to service their debts.
2 To improve quality and productivity, firms in the region need to shed excessive labour. Funding rising unemployment, as well as paying extra social security to an ageing population, is, necessarily, a very difficult task for governments. If they tax profits, it damages investment; if they borrow, it raises taxes; if they tax heavily, it discourages initiative and entrepreneurship.
3 To achieve export success, these countries must be allowed access to Western European markets. The impact on unemployment in the EU steel industry of extra competition from Czech and Polish steel steelmakers is already a subject for debate.

The difficulties are compounded by the fact that, economically and politically, there is no way back to autarkic socialism for these countries. They must take the path towards social market economics and constitutional democracy and they must do it resolutely. This means change – in attitudes, practices and jobs for workers and managers. It is not going to be easy but it will be done.

Further reading

Abell, D. and Kollermeier, T. (eds), *Dynamic Entrepreneurship in Central and Eastern Europe*, EFER, Amsterdam, 1992.
Cascio, W. F., *Managing Human Resources*, McGraw-Hill, Maidenhead, 1992.
IMD and World Economic Forum, *Emerging Market Economies Report 1993*, Lausanne, 1993.
IMD and World Economic Forum, *The World Competitiveness Report 1993*, Lausanne, 1993.
Jackson, M. *et al.* (eds), *Systems Thinking in Europe*, Plenum Press, New York, 1991.
Kaltnekar, Z. (ed.), *Organization and Information Systems*, Proceedings of OIS International Conference, Bled, 1992.
Porter, M., *The Competitive Advantage of Nations*, Free Press, New York, 1990.
Srica, V., *Principles of Management*, Zagreb Business School (in Croatian), Zagreb, 1992.

6 Managing people in Scandinavia

Kurt H. Parkum and Flemming Agersnap

Scandinavia includes the individual countries of Denmark, Norway and Sweden which have common characteristics, including similarities in language, culture, history and geographic location. Sometimes Finland and Iceland are also included, although culture and language are quite different. Yet these two countries have in former times been part of the three other countries, and they have been influenced by their culture.

The following review and discussion will focus upon that part of Scandinavia which is represented by Norway, Sweden and Denmark. Reference will also be made to Finland.

While the Scandinavian countries were united as one country under Queen Margaret I (1375–1412), they have been independent countries since then, with the exception of Norway, which was part of first, Denmark and then Sweden! Several earlier conflicts with the Germans, especially a Danish defeat by the Prussians in 1864, along with controversies among the Scandinavian countries, may in part account for the fact that the culture of these countries developed differently from that of their large neighbours to the south. However, there are also cultural differences within the Scandinavian countries. Historic divergences in the developments of the countries as well as geographic differences and a different industrial base may help to explain that the countries differ in spite of many cultural similarities.

Denmark: history and main political and economic features

Denmark adopted a liberal constitution in 1849 and achieved a democratic parliamentary government some fifty years later in 1901. A few years later an alliance of Social Democrats and Radical Liberals came to power, and the character of Danish politics began to emerge. The Social Democrats has been the largest political party up to the present time.

While Denmark maintained a policy of neutrality up to the Second World War it abandoned it after the war and joined NATO as well as the Council of Europe and EFTA. In 1973 it left EFTA and joined the EC.

The Danish population of about 5.1 million people is very homogeneous. Foreign citizens make up only 3.3 per cent of the population. The country is a welfare state with high standards of education and health care. The majority of the population is nominally Lutheran, the state religion. There is complete religious freedom.

In 1990 the largest domestic product was government services (24 per cent), mining and manufacturing was second (19 per cent), miscellaneous private services third (16 per cent), wholesale and retail trade next (14 per cent). Other domestic production includes transport and communications, building and construction, agriculture and forestry, as well as banking and insurance. Oil and gas production began in 1972, and Denmark met 70 per cent of domestic energy requirements in 1990. Cheese, tinned meat, cereals, and pork and bacon are the leading agricultural export products.

The manufacturing industry in Denmark is characterized by diversity and a large number of mostly small firms. Dominant products are food processing, pharmaceutical products and furniture. Other services are engineering, tourism and shipping. Over two-thirds of Denmark's merchandise export earnings are from the sale of manufactured goods, including engineering products.

Norway: history and main political and economic features

Norway's history is bound up with that of Denmark and Sweden. Between 1450 and 1814 the country was under Danish rule and between 1814 and 1905 subject to the Swedish king but with extensive 'home rule'. Norway has been an independent country since 1905, except for the period of German occupation from 1940 to 1945.

Apart from this occupation period, a Labour government held power between 1905 and 1965, when a non-socialistic coalition government was elected. This remained in power until 1971, when a minority Labour administration took office. The Labour Party is the largest, although its size diminished during the 1980s, and the Conservative Party is the second largest (22 per cent). There are an additional six smaller parties in Parliament (the *Storting*). As in the other Nordic countries, considerable stress is traditionally placed on consensus formation in politics. The Norwegian parliament, like the Danish, is organized on the basis of proportional representation. There are mandatory elections every four years.

Although Norway has applied for EC membership twice, the population voted both times not to join (in 1962 and 1967), and it still remains outside the EU pending the result of its third application. Norway has been a member of NATO since 1949. Furthermore, like Sweden, Denmark, Finland and Iceland, it is a member of the Nordic Council and a common market for labour. Norway has also been a member of the European Free Trade Association (EFTA) since 1960, as well as several other European organizations (CSCE and OECD).

The population was about 4.3 million in 1992, and it is very homogeneous. Norway has a high standard of living and a deep cross-party commitment to welfare provisions since the Second World War.

Although outside the EU the Norwegian currency (krone) is linked to the European Monetary Union. Yet Norway experienced a devaluation of about 10 per cent in 1992. The country has a liberal free market economy, although some large companies, especially in energy areas, are wholly or partly state owned. The economy is strong, even if it started to reflect the global economic downturn in 1991. Real GDP growth has remained high (1.9 per cent per year in 1991). Full employment has been a priority since 1945, and unemployment is low (5.5 per cent in 1991), although it is on the increase.

Oil and gas production was started in 1971, and this has strengthened the economy. The country became a net exporter of oil during the mid-1970s, and production has been growing since. Norway is now the largest oil exporter in Europe, and this area has increasingly become the base for the country's economy. However, hydroelectric power is the major source of energy for Norway's own use.

The business sector is one of the most heavily subsidized in the OECD, especially in agriculture. The largest contributors to the GDP in 1990 are public services (16 per cent), manufacturing, mining and quarrying (15 per cent), oil production and pipeline transport (13 per cent), and wholesale and retail trade (10 per cent). Other smaller sectors include transport and communications, dwellings, construction, financial services, electricity, agriculture, forestry and fishing, as well as ocean transport and oilwell drilling. The country is self-sufficient in meat, fish, potatoes and dairy products. It is an importer of cereals. The importance of fishing has been reduced during the past 20 years, due partly to rapid expansion of other sectors and partly to fishing-resource constraints.

A significant part of manufacturing involves the processing and added value to Norway's natural resources, mainly the mineral and power resources but also fish products, wood products, furniture and paper. In recent years there has been a steady decline in the investment goods sector. The most important subsector in manufacturing is engineering, although its importance has been declining. Construction accounts for more than half of gross fixed capital formation, in spite of the fact that this area since 1988 has been hard hit by the recession. Shipping is another major area in that the merchant navy represents over 10 per cent of world tonnage.

Sweden: history and main political and economic features

Sweden was at one point in its early history under Danish control, but it was liberated from Danish possession in the sixteenth century. It subsequently went through a period of considerable expansion, and Swedish kings were during one period of its history in control of the areas around the Baltic sea including Finland. Finland became a semi-autonomous state under the Russian Czar until 1917, when it became fully independent. It fought against the USSR in the Second World War. It succeeded in keeping its status as an independent state but had to make considerable accommodation to Soviet policy. Sweden was neutral during the Second World War.

The Swedish economy is characterized by a highly developed industrial sector, which evolved from the country's natural resources. The main part of the GDP is distributed as follows: government services, etc. 29 per cent, manufacturing 21 per cent, financing, insurance and other business services 18 per cent, wholesale and retail trade, hotels, etc. 11 per cent. The remaining part of the GDP is composed of areas that each make only small additional contributions. They include construction, transportation, communications and various services. Agriculture, forestry, fishing, mining, etc. combined represent no more than 3 per cent of the GDP.

The Swedish advanced social welfare system is internationally famous and is based upon the concept of social development in a mixed economy. An extensive welfare system includes a system of state-organized insurance programmes.

The main division in Swedish politics has been between a labour bloc, mainly the Social Democrats, committed to the distribution of wealth and a strong public sector, and a non-socialistic bloc consisting of the Conservative, Centre and Liberal Parties. These latter parties were opposed to the social democratic programme, and they were finally able to form a coalition government in the 1970s. Although by far the largest party, the Social Democrats have not been able to regain their previous popularity. Government tends to alternate between two sets of coalitions.

A comparison among the Scandinavian countries

The Scandinavian countries would, on a continuum from a *laissez-faire* orientation to a centralized political orientation, be closer to the *laissez-faire*-oriented UK than to the centralized political orientation of France.[1] The Scandinavian countries exemplify those that were industrialized later than most other European nations and without much direct intervention from the state, as was the case in Germany.

There is throughout Scandinavia a strong tradition of union membership and influence, and almost all employees belong to unions. There is also a tradition of collective agreements without legislative backing, except when both management and labour have wanted legislation. There is also a strong tradition for industrial democracy at the company level. It is the law that firms with more than 25 employees must have worker–management collaboratives and 50 per cent management representatives. One of the latter group must be a representative of middle management.

In addition, one-third of the members of the board of directors of stock-owned companies must represent the employees of the company. It is also worth noting that about 30 per cent of publicly owned stocks in companies throughout Scandinavia is owned by institutional investors such as pension funds, insurance companies and financial institutions such as banks.

Lindkvist[2] concludes on the basis of conversations with Scandinavian researchers and management consultants that culture and assumptions are strongly connected to a common historic development. The main point seems to be that this common background is also mentioned as a major factor. The specific result is an emphasis in Scandinavia on equality and consensus. Management operates within a cultural framework that is based upon strong cooperation and a high degree of unionization. Terms such as the 'Nordic welfare model' and the 'Nordic social model' are mentioned along with the Protestant ethic and an emphasis upon consensus democracy. The countries are also characterized by geographic proximity, a shared history and former union, the shared cultural heritage, and three similar languages, easily understood by people from the other Scandinavian countries. (The Finnish language, however, is very different.) Other cultural similarities are probably associated with a common Protestant state religion; a set of legal principles based more on Nordic and Germanic than Roman law; peaceful relations; political stability; constitutionally assured democracies; a non-competitive stance towards other nations; highly developed levels of engineering sciences and technology, and equal opportunity. These variables can all be assumed to have an influence upon Scandinavian management practices.[3]

Schramm-Nielsen,[4] editor of a powerful collection of articles on management in Scandinavia, points out that the Scandinavian countries have reached comparable levels of technical and economic development. If it can be assumed that cultures tend to converge as a result of such similarities, then this would help to account for a uniformity in attitudes and values. It is pointed out, however, that people felt shared fundamental cultural values even during periods when Nordic countries did not have similar levels of technical and economic development. In any case the cultural communality seems to be beyond questioning.

Management style

Sweden

It is pointed out by Lawrence and Spybey,[5] as part of a discussion of the context and style of Swedish management, that industrialization in Sweden, when it came, was quick and effective, and that it was invention-driven.

They suggest that the consequences are that the Swedes equate industrialization with modernization and see it as the key to affluence. The results are that it is very acceptable to be working in industry, and that industrial managers in Sweden are perceived as being both energetic and able. Swedish managers are, as a rule, very well educated.

The undifferentiated nature of society is exemplified by (1) equality between men and women, (2) slight class differences, although education, job status and income does make a difference, and (3) narrow income differences, what Lawrence and Spybey refer to as 'a cult of competence in Sweden, and correspondingly no amateur point of view; those that do not know keep quiet, and let those that do get on with the job at hand'.

Lawrence and Spybey find management, like the Swedish society, to be quite redistributive. They note that the links between management and society are particularly strong. The values of egalitarianism, neutralism and welfare are all felt to have an impact on management features in Swedish society. The emphasis upon egalitarianism, according to Lawrence and Spybey, (1) precludes authoritarian management styles, (2) precludes a 'them and us' mentality in industry, (3) facilitates communication, both vertical and lateral, and (4) is a prerequisite for the operation of co-determination or industrial democracy.

The organizational structure of Swedish corporations is often perceived by foreign managers as ambiguous. There is a preference for matrix structures and for overlapping reporting systems. Such managers will claim that the decision-making process is long and diffuse, and the visibility of the process is poor. They perceive unclear objectives, and some even feel that management is indecisive and slow. They feel that it is even difficult to recognize it when decisions have in fact been made.[6]

Relations between foreign subsidiaries and their Swedish headquarters are not very formal. Control is also informal, implicit but still very compelling. There is a tendency to seek consensus and a desire to avoid confrontations. Difficult and embarrassing situations are avoided. Feedback is very clear, but corrective action against poor performers is exceptional. Authority is usually not exercised solely on the basis of formal power.

At the heart of the Swedish industrial democracy, according to Lawrence and Spybey, is the concept of the right to negotiate. Worker representatives have the right to raise issues, to discuss with management, to negotiate, to seek agreement, and if this agreement is not achieved, to negotiate at higher levels all the way to the national level.

Industrial democracy is not only widely accepted, it is also seen as a means of buying industrial peace and harmony in negotiations. However, Lawrence and Spybey point to the possibility that management initiatives are delayed or repressed as a result of the potential controversy associated with expected scrutiny by worker representatives.

Lawrence and Spybey describe Swedish managers as mild-mannered, ready to listen and discuss, restrained in their behaviour, temperate in their judgement, rational and disinclined to engage in conflict. They are slow to make decisions, apparently because they consider it counter to norms of reasonableness and humility to appear to hustle colleagues and subordinates into making decisions. This approach appears to facilitate the eventual implementation of the decisions.

Denmark

Danish companies are, on average, smaller than in Sweden, and this appears to influence the management style. Lawrence and Spybey observe that Danish managers would claim to be more pragmatic and less systems-driven than the Swedes. The Danes see themselves as less impersonal and less serious-minded, as having a special sense of ironic humour. Rightly or wrongly, remarks which Danes ascribe to such humour are at times perceived by foreigners as a form for hostility. Schramm-Nielsen[4] agrees that foreigners tend to feel that the Danish humour is impolite and aggressive, and that the Danes would be wise to keep it to themselves. She softens the impression of the Danish attitude, however, by suggesting that the irony has an implication of solidarity, and that it is a 'laugh-with-humour' which implies consensus and togetherness rather than distance and conflict.

At the same time, there seems to be an attitude similar to that of the Japanese, who have the saying 'the nail that sticks out will be hammered down'. The Danish version takes the form of the so-called 'Jante law', so named by Sandemose, a Danish–Norwegian author. The idea is to discourage excellence, or as Sandemose puts it: 'Don't think you are special, don't think you are worth as much as we are, don't think you are wiser than we are, and don't think you are better than we are.' It is not surprising than some Danes as individuals tend to understate their abilities, competence and intelligence.

Such modesty is not widespread, however, when it comes to an assessment of the national contribution of Danish culture, science and the few individual Danes (mostly deceased) who have managed to be recognized in spite of the Jante law. Those who most strongly express pride in this regard may psychologically represent the case of inflation that naturally goes with feelings of inferiority. On the other hand, there are definitely cases where national pride in achievements are quite appropriate.

The educational system is a major socializing agent, and the Danish system is egalitarian. This is probably due in part to the considerable influence which the Danish parson and author Nicolaj Grundtivg (1783–1872) has played in the shaping of Danish cultural life. There is, furthermore, an emphasis upon values which downplay competition while making a special effort to preparing pupils to active participation in a democratic society.[4]

The educational system for business and especially for future managers has been developed and differentiated over the years. Yet it is kept as one system so that a young person can enter at trade school and continue to the highest academic levels. Students with a more comprehensive background may enter at a higher level if they wish to add a business degree to their education. Examples would be students with an academic high school education or an engineering degree. Compared, for example, with the UK, a far greater percentage of business students achieve advanced business degrees by attending either day or evening programmes. An advanced business curriculum will normally comprise a broad range of subjects. In addition to trade subjects it would include, for example, behavioural science and macroeconomics.

Schramm-Nielsen[4] also points to a Danish preference for egalitarianism, managerial discretion, responsibility and confidence in one another. Several points from her summary of Danish preferences are worth noting in this context. The Danes prefer an informal and direct mode of association; pay as little attention as possible to rank and status; usually prefer an informal way of addressing other people; are informal in the clothes they wear; and they attach importance to being 'natural'. Fashion, of course, changes over time and from setting to setting. Danes who dress informally in office situations can be surprisingly well dressed at, for example, dinner parties and theatre visits. The current overall trend seems to be toward more formal dressing norms.[4]

The following characteristics of Danish management are also applicable to other Nordic countries; tolerance of uncertainty; small power distance; a favourable attitude towards new ideas; contact seeking; the concept that small is beautiful; orientation towards harmony; pragmatism; and an ability to change easily from pleasantry to seriousness. However, there are negative aspects to a Danish management style which are also valid. The characterization would then focus upon the following words, which are quite negative; scared; unprincipled; slow; conflict avoiding; comfortable; conformity seeking; as well as chatting and joking. On balance, however, the positive description seems best to capture the essence.[7]

The study by Hofstede indicates that there is a little power distance among people in Denmark. This translates in an organizational setting into a preference for flat organizations with a sliding transition of authority. The preference is to delegate authority, de-emphasize control and to invite participation in decision making.[4]

Egalitarianism is valued in a managerial context, as in society at large. It follows that the question who has authority over whom is replaced with the question of who is responsible for what. Subordinates may have their way, and it is acceptable to make mistakes. As a result, there is little concern about showing respect and agreeing with a supervisor. It is the result that counts rather than personal relationships.

Decision making, according to Schramm-Nielsen,[4] is usually delegated to a large number of people, all of whom can make decisions within their area of responsibility. Thus authority, power to make decisions (responsibility, in other words) are all the prerogative of a large number of people in a given organization. The Danes prefer the term 'delegation of responsibility' to 'delegation of authority' or 'delegation of power'.

Danish managers tend to work methodically and in a structured way. They generally spend a great deal of time in meetings where they seek pragmatic solutions. They value an empirically rational approach to problems, and they tend to be action and goal-oriented. However, they tend to spend relatively little time analysing a problem before they proceed to making a decision.[4] This observation is supported by a small study of Danish companies,[8] which concludes that the Danes seem to be behind other Europeans in adopting planning to their business. Instead of setting up very formal planning systems they try to keep the planning process flexible and informal. There is a strong aversion to over-engineering the process and becoming technique-bound, too 'gimmicky' or too quantitative. Paperwork is kept to a minimum. Instead the Danes tend to emphasize visionary, creative and conceptual thinking at the expense of more formal, quantitative analysis.

Norway

Norwegian management values can be summarized as follows: informal structures are important and authority is always subject to renegotiation. While these are the main points, some additional observations are added. It is suggested by Andersen[9] that management is characterized by authority based upon competence; that organizations possess a weak orientation towards results; that there is much latitude for a closed 'clique mentality' at the managerial level; and finally, that the oil industry constitutes a counter-culture to the other aspects of Norwegian culture. The differences that are specific to the oil industry are primarily: a strong emphasis upon formal role specification; less latitude for negotiating authoritative decisions; and a strong result orientation.[2]

Finland

The Finns tend to be conscious about their own culture. The Finns have a feeling of security with their own citizens but insecurity in relation to foreigners. While individualism is high at a personal level, there tends to be consensus at a societal level. Finally, emotions and reason are seen as parallel.[10]

In negotiations the Finns are seen as being attentive and taking the other party seriously. They are also reputed to be flexible and willing to act at short notice. Finally, they respect knowledge and this means that research and development are taken seriously. It also means that education is respected and is seen as a good way to achieve a high position in a business setting or elsewhere.[2]

Conclusions

The preceding review of Nordic management has emphasized differences which in the final analysis are comparatively minor. On the whole it is fair to say that similarities outweigh the differences. As the above shows, there is a long tradition of democracy and a humanitarian attitude, and the approach to management mirrors that. Managers in Scandinavia are primarily occupied with an organic outlook. The organization is regarded as a whole. Too much attention to sub-goals is discouraged.

There is also a preference for goals which are agreed upon within the organization compared with those forced upon the company from the outside. Industrial democracy is widely practised as demonstrated by the fact that the ideas and opinions of all the employees are taken into account and are taken seriously.[11]

The above observations refer to all of Scandinavia, and any attempt to focus upon the differences among the individual Nordic countries should be understood as comparatively minor compared with the prominent historical and cultural similarities. The differences which can be identified from the above review of the literature are summarized below. However, it is in the nature of a brief summary in that it constitutes a stereotyped and simplified description. It is nonetheless an indication of the differences which the literature seems to indicate.

- The Norwegians are proud and concerned about being provincial. They tend to downplay their roles as managers.
- The Finns tend to appear passive and take the role of the listener. Their observations are well considered and often essential when they finally do speak. They are known for endurance and reliability.
- The Danes are considered tough in regard to industrial relations negotiations. Their philosophy is that they want something in return whenever they give up something.
- Swedish managers are considered flexible and easily adaptable to foreign cultures and peoples. They are also systematic and careful planners.

It can be seen that an overall conclusion must include both differences and similarities. Most Scandinavians would probably agree with a widespread perception among other Europeans that the similarities in the final analysis outweigh the differences.

References

1 Grønbaek, D., *Industripolitik i Danmark og Sverige*, Politiske Studier, Copenhagen, 1991.
2 Lindkvist, L., *A Passionate Search for Nordisk Management*, (unpublished) IOA, Copenhagen, 1988, pp. 1–75.
3 McFate, 1984.
4 Schram-Nielsen, J., *Management in Scandinavia, Differences and Similarities*, SPRøK, 1991.
5 Lawrence, P. and Spybey, T., *Management and Society in Sweden*, Routledge and Kegan Paul, London, 1986.
6 Forss, K., Hawk, D. and Hedlund, G., *Cultural Differences – Swedishness in Legislation, Multinational Corporations and Aid Administrations*, IIB, Stockholm, 1985.
7 Agersnap, F. and Larsen, B., *Dansk Ledelse?* Harvard Børsen, 22, 1987.
8 Ackelsberg, R. and Harris, W. C., 'How Danish companies plan', *Long Range Planning*, **22**, 6, 111–116.
9 Andersen, S. S., *Seks Teser om Organisasjon og Ledelse i Norske Bedrifter*, Bedriftsøkonomisk Institutt, Oslo, 1988.
10 Laine-Sveiby, K., *National Kultur som Strategi*, Eva, Helsingfors, 1987.
11 Czarniawska, B. and Wolf, R., 'How we decide and how we act – on the assumptions of Viking organization theory', in Wolf, R. (ed.), *Organising Industrial Development*, Walter de Gruyter, Berlin, 1986, p. 284.

Further reading

Denmark, Iceland Country Profile 1992–93, The Economist Intelligence Unit, London, 1992, pp. 1–29.
Norway Country Profile 1992–93, The Economist Intelligence Unit, London, 1992.
Sweden Country Profile, The Economist Intelligence Unit, London, 1992–1993.

7 Managing people in Russia
Terry Garrison and Anton Artemyev

Introduction

It is important to recognize at the outset the precise extent to which current human resources management in Russia, along with other features of management practice, have been significantly affected – if not substantially constrained – by the country's previous centralized economic and political system. True, the recent politico-economic reforms and the switch from Soviet to Russian state ownership of the vast proportion of the country's large-scale factories and commercial undertakings, still publicly owned and employing the great majority of the workers, have made some difference to the nature of the state/industry interface. This applies particularly to all organizations which can take advantage of the current relaxation of centrist controls and legal changes that stem from the Gorbachov–Yeltsin reforms at Russian and CIS levels (e.g. in matters of creating links with Western companies or freedom to hold Western currency). Naturally, also, sole traders or collectives or privatized companies which are now not state-owned have had autonomy to operate as they wish since the start of the reform period. But, equally naturally, the country's heavy industry and important branches of Russia's military–industrial complex are still subject to statutory linkages with the centre, covering industrial financing and integrated planning for example, which predate *perestroika*. This is evidenced by the moves made by the Russian Central Bank, under the control of the Congress of Peoples' Deputies over the period 1990–1993. These involved increasing the subsidization of state industry (i.e. to continue to pay wages, maintain full employment and cover losses without necessary regard to the profitability of enterprises) during the slump in manufacturing activity.

The fact of the 'de-ministration' of Russian industry is also important in this discussion. Here, as a consequence of the reforms since 1985, the previous relationships between individual enterprises in a given branch of industry (say, steel or cars) and the all-union industrial ministry, which supervised the activities of all the firms in that branch, have been either dismantled or significantly changed. As the state planning and supply systems (GOSPLAN and GOSNAB) ceased to function, so also major enterprises were freed from tight ministerial tutelage. Hence, their previously unavoidable duty to contribute to the financing of a set of bureaucratic monoliths whose role was that of controlling Soviet production has ceased.

This has also had its downside for state-owned industry, as the creation in the early 1990s of the Civic Party Union shows. This was a political grouping of many of the interests involved with state firms and contained many directors/managers who were opposed to continuation of the reform process in its present form. Consequently, many of the larger state-owned companies have in fact more operational freedom and less state protection (due to de-ministration) than before but are directed by those who sometimes wish for more. Even with the implantation of democratic reforms in late 1993, the December election, this ethos still persists.

Thus there are many companies in Russia who are still greatly affected by the statutory and organizational effects of Russia's politico-economic system – some because they wish to be – and a growing number, who, because of the reforms, are less dependent on systemic vestiges from the past. The nearer an enterprise is to trade dependence on the West and the more pronounced its interest in hard currency, the more it seems – on current evidence – to value whatever autonomy it has. And to value it greatly.

If we were to examine on a more micro level the influences which the system has exercised in the human resource management area, we should need to consider such elements are Marx's Labour Theory of Value. We should also need to understand the recognition by all Russian governments since Lenin's of the need to maintain full employment, as a matter of fact and not just political oratory, for reasons of Communist ideology. Both of these, as we shall see later, have left such an imprint on the Russian worker as to have become implicit in the management systems of all large firms, whatever their relationship with the state. This micro influence on Russian commerce and industry is, in fact, so pervasive and deep-seated that it poses many problems for the regeneration of the Russian economy. For many workers in Russia *perestroika* is shorthand for mass unemployment.

Aspects of the human resource management system

It is interesting that, although each enterprise always had a personnel management department, there was no special ministry at a central government level covering all related issues. This, in what was a planned economy, may be seen as a considerable anomaly. The policy of managing the labour resource as a factor of production in quantitative terms was, however, enunciated – and implemented – by each ministry in conjunction with large enterprises in its sector or branch. Issues of pay and productivity, of capital investment and worker participation were thus centrally addressed at governmental level.

It is also interesting for the Western observer to note that the personnel management system for firms in Russia, as a system, was and still is technically more sophisticated than one could expect and covers all issues from collecting and processing information on job vacancies, planning how to meet future workforce requirements – the workforce used to be typically referred to as the workers' collective (*trudovoy kollectiv*) – and work study on different production operations. The redesign of output-related wage systems, executive interviewing/training and career development are also standard.

Three peculiarities of the system need to be considered. The first is the level to which the system was (and is) heavily technocratic and quantity-orientated. It still emphasizes the technical side of the production/commercial problem to be faced rather than its more human dimensions. In so doing, it has many similarities to the nineteenth-century German approach to the technocratic management of industrial systems from which Russian industrialization drew much inspiration and not a few models. The Western observer at the start of the 1990s cannot fail to be struck in Russia by the importance attached by companies to managers' verifiable technical/scientic/technological expertise. 'Thing management' takes precedence over 'people management'. The Communist system was constructed, from the first, as a input–output system which conerned itself with physical supply relationships and took little (if no) account of the vagaries of human behaviour, especially marketplace demand. Indeed, GOSPLAN recognized neither demand nor, for that matter, the marketplace.

This is not to say that the Soviet system did not recognize individual effort. It certainly did and, in fact, rewarded outstanding achievement with official recognition at all-union and government levels (Hero of the Soviet Union, Hero of Socialist Labour, etc.) and at plant level. Here the rewards for contribution were recognition ('Stakhanovite worker'), badges and medals and official mention on the firm's special 'honour board'. In their time these proxy indicators of productivity were highly valued as motivators. On the other hand, concepts of individual performance rewards (bonus payments) and the relationship of individual pay for quality work or even level of service were not elements which attracted similar attention. If anything, the typical Soviet approach was to dissociate material rewards from the psychic gain of contributing powerfully to the construction of Socialism.

Excessive individualism, and the materialism that it might connote, were not tolerable in industrial enterprises wherever they visibly detracted from the concept of group solidarity and social equality. Thus some of the incentives available to managers in Western firms (in the form of performance-related pay, for example) were not available in Russia in anything like the same form or to the same extent. They would hardly have been of value, anyway, to non-*apparatchiks* since the system as a whole – over the entire Communist rule period with the exception of the New Economic Policy in the 1920s – was producing hardly any goods (cars, dwellings, etc.) which were suited to Western-style conspicuous consumption.

The ultimate goal of all the plans of successive Soviet governments related always to volume of output, a fact that stamped a consistent production orientation on all facets of commercial life. As any Western shopper at GUM in Moscow or Gostiny Dvor in St Petersburg can testify, even the most basic of marketing notions are today utterly alien to the great majority of Russian retail personnel. For them a high standard of service to a valued customer tends to equate with a feeling of subservience or even servility to an undesirable irritating supplicant, who happens to be patiently standing in a queue. This is such a business pathology that it amounts to not just a production orientation but a form of anti-marketing.

Perhaps this is understandable, even justifiable, in terms of the almost exclusive stress laid since Stalinist times in Russia on heavy industry and defence-related requirements to the almost total exclusion (in Western eyes) of consumer products. But even so, it will require substantial remedial change in a managerial approach, which has traditionally regarded employees as merely 'resources' and supply (and not demand) as all-important, for marketing to have meaning. In fact, it was only in the late 1980s that the term 'human resources' began to come into vogue in the business sector. Clearly, a marketing orientation for businesses will only truly come into existence when staff themselves are valued properly, as individuals.

The second aspect of this peculiarity was the extent to which labour was regarded as a commodity whose cost was seen as a macroeconomic variable to be managed centrally – at ministry level. Thus wages were set for the workers in a particular factory centrally by government ministries who themselves, through their industry-wide planning system, were imposing production targets on the same factory. The sense of alienation produced by a factory manager's inability to manage his or her tasks 'in the round' was profound and is responsible for much of the gross inattention to quality and detailed customer requirements from which Soviet industry suffered and which still desperately needs to be changed. Responsibility for all aspects of an enterprise's industrial performance could not be specifically located within the individual enterprise itself. Therefore, provided the factory fulfilled its output targets within the plan, its management did not need to concern themselves overmuch with qualitative success criteria.

This failing in the system made the quantitative approach to the management of labour referred to above considerably worse in its effects on the individual worker. The dominant factor for the system as a whole was the extent of decreasing unit labour costs as the factories were, under the plan, obliged to seek increasing utilization of their labour. The workers simply had no incentives – beyond that of loyal membership of a section, brigade or department of their company and a possible wish to contribute to the success of the USSR's political system – to inspire them to commitment. Faced only with quantitative targets and knowing that, whatever happened, their jobs were secure, workers knew they did not have to produce quality products. After all, was not the purpose of GOSPLAN to eliminate competition among producers by dismantling the marketplace?

The command economy also dealt with the issue of the supply of workers by regulating the mobility of workers. If workers were needed for the construction of a new factory in Siberia or Donbass, they were supplied as required. The critical element was the subordination of all aspects of the human resources management process to GOSPLAN demands. Recent, pre-Yeltsin reforms – such as the Law on the State Enterprise – were seeking to come to terms with the rigidities in central planning and Russian management thinking that such approaches almost literally cemented in place.

Difficulties that occurred as a result at plant level were not far to seek. Staff received pay for work whose economic value was not calculated and were managed by administrators whose task was simply to meet volume production targets. Because of the centralized labour supply system, workforces were, in a way, statutorily attached to their enterprises. As a result, the typical problem was the conflict between the administration wishing to retain its workforce and disaffected workers wishing to leave, but being unable to do so. Several measures to support the factory administration's control over its workforce were introduced by the state. Among them one should be mentioned as the most severe (Stalinist) restriction: to forbid workers to leave their designated place of work in a specific enterprise.

The legacy of such factors is a widespread aversion to risk and a lack of entrepreneurial feeling on the part of Russian managers and workers alike.

Impact of history

There are three major historical elements which have influenced, over time, the shaping of the human resource management system in Russia. They are the state, the Church and the commercial culture.

The Russian national character has been shaped by many influences. In the past – and bearing in mind the system of communications – Russia's mere size and geography made any form of central decision making and standardized rule impossible, unless it were utterly coercive. Indeed, the very pattern of widely spaced city settlement in Russia makes economies of scale in the distribution of consumer products from a central manufacturing facility difficult to realize. This has major implications for foreign consumer product companies now seeking to implant in Russia.

The history of Russia, prior to the Communist Revolution, is a history of despotism – sometimes benevolent, sometimes harsh, but always autocratic. The major result was a brand of feudalism involving rigid patterns of social stratification based on differences in ownership, especially – as in France – of land. Even afterwards, the history of Russia was not dissimilar, until the Gorbachov era, since the party and its *apparatchiks* formed a new type of aristocracy under a leader whose tendencies almost inevitably were towards autocracy.

Politically, the country has always been a melting-pot of different races, religions, languages and cultures, held together since the earliest days of empire under Ivan the Terrible more by the fact of empire and fear of authority than economic or political realities. Now, many of the political problems associated with the breakdown of central rule (separatism, independence, civil war and even the growth in criminality, etc.) are familar to Western observers as part of the decolonization process which accompanies the end of empire and the removal of overt repression. It should be noted that Russia never enjoyed the economic uplift which the possession of colonies gave to, say, Britain. Nor did it enjoy the democratic perspectives which management of a disparate empire gave the British. The Russian Empire was not renowned for its tolerance.

The absence of any democracy worthy of the name for the whole of Russia's recorded history – until now – is a further element in this jigsaw. In no other European country was the precise pattern of Russian 'feudalism', involving explicit social ranking based on monarchical/aristocratic peasant patterns of unequal wealth and land ownership, maintained into the twentieth century. The concepts stemming from serfdom were hard to eradicate in a country where a bourgeois class was relatively small and widely dispersed in the major centres of population. Under Communism, of course, every attempt was made to eradicate bourgeois thinking – with its emphasis on making and keeping money, on acquiring and maintaining property ownership – in order to achieve social equalization of the worker classes.

It is important, also, to recognize that many features of Russia's economic mechanism were formed specifically according to a model which differs from Western ones. Russia was unique among the major European nations as, until quite recent times, solely a land power. Its pattern of economic development was one of extensive prospecting of the rich Russian hinterland (coal, oil, diamonds, etc.) and heavy selective industrialization to build up a strong political and economic infrastructure. It was not that of seeking the typical Western balance of an economy orientated equally to the output of consumption and investment goods, involving the ownership and exploitation of overseas colonies. Democratic political pressures to help shape market demand never existed in Communist times.

Table 7.1 *The Russian business culture: iceberg–bedrock features*

Element of difference	UK	Russia
Key influence on political economic thinking	Sea power	Land power
Nature of government experience	Democratic since 1215	Feudal and totalitarian up to late 1980s
Timing of industrialization	Early	Late
Timing of embourgeoisement	Early	No middle class exists in any Western sense
Growth of democratic Institutions	Early establishment of parliamentary system	Institutions set up in early 1990s
Dominant social philosophy derived from	Protestantism, capitalism	Russian orthodoxy and feudalism/Communism
Power base	Colonial empire	Continental rule
Internal distances	Short	Long
Trade and industry development	T → I	I → T
Key social orientation	Individual competition	Group cooperation
Key economic orientation	Liberalism	Collectivism
Direct recent experience of political unrest and military destruction	Slight	Massive

Finally, the economic evolution of Russia was based on the development of land- as opposed to seaborne trade. This had, and has, important implications for the country's receptivity to new ideas for economic management and its access to foreign consumer products. Russia never had the overseas colonies, with all the attendant economic advantages and political worries, that (for example) the French enjoyed. They never had the pineapples, either! (See Table 7.1.)

The vision from Moscow was always more circumscribed. Indeed, merchanting and trading in Russia was historically a relatively restricted affair, confined, that is, to certain families, groups or companies in the major cities. The small size and island nature of Britain made seaborne trade for all its citizens an everyday reality. The Russian population as a whole was never exposed to this extent of commercial thinking and behaviour, especially those who were in the remoter agricultural or mining areas. One of the Russian words for 'market' is *Yarmark*. This derives from medieval times when, for many agriculturalists, there was only one opportunity to buy many manufactured goods – the yearly market or, as in German, *Jahrmarkt*.

It is important, too, to recognize the lack of a financial services infrastructure and a wide-ranging commercial value system in Russia and the extent to which this is rooted in history. The impact on Russia of similar thinking to that behind the Catholic Church's doctrine on usury (Gratian's *decretum* of 1141) and papal supremacy (Boniface VIII's *Unam Sanctam*) among leaders of the Orthodox Church and Tsardom was to strictly limit the sound acceptability of commercial thinking.

It is interesting to speculate that the rise in the power of Mafia-type gangs to control the country's huge black market is as much due to the shortcomings of the command–administrative economy (i.e. in not supplying consumer goods) as it is to the lack of a trading instinct in a broad swathe of its population.

This last element – the allegedly uncommercial nature of much of Russian society – can be examined more closely from the perspective of religion. Such a viewpoint again throws into sharper relief aspects of the conceptual framework within which human resource management in Russia must be seen. Two factors are of importance.

The first is the extent to which Russia did not share in some of the cultural values which were ultimately derived from the classical philosophies of Greece and Rome. This is especially relevant in terms of the extent to which the Russian Orthodox Church promoted concepts of the desirability of an ordered, collective existence which were at variance with the West's comparative espousal of individualistic freedoms. As a result, substantial stress was laid on social interdependence, on a community's acceptance of the divine ordering of the world and on the personal moral responsibility and discipline needed. In the face of manifold religious/secular rules governing all aspects of life, all societal structures evolved patterns of subservience and obedience – to the bishop, the landowner (or *hoziayin*), the ranking civil servant. Russia developed in its people strains both of fatalism (accepting God's will) and introversion ('Russia's ways are best') which, at key times in its history, were in sharp contrast (and often conflict) with the ideas of those 'modernizers' who wished to reorientate society and the economy to the West. Peter I – founder of St Petersburg – was one such ruler who sought this end. Even today, this schism is still evident.

The second is the way in which the Church politically buttressed the existence of an absolute monarchy, and vice versa. The sanctity of the Tsar, as a divinely appointed ruler, could only be maintained if, in fact, the Tsar himself upheld the central position of the Russian Orthodox Church. This had important implications for the workings of the Russian economy from its earliest days, when, as the particular result of Church strictures on the sin of money lending, as we noted, Russia failed to develop a workable credit/banking system of its own. Industry was long held back through this; a merchanting mentality failed to develop in the Russian people – a paradox, since the first Kievan state had been founded by Norse traders; the manufacture (at Tula) of weapons and other strategic commodities became closely controlled by the state.

Did not Communist ideology take the place of the Church in buttressing the existence of the party's successive leaders, in much the same way?

The sense of societal cohesion and the impact of collective values is nowhere more evident than in the Russians' response to its enemies in the last two centuries. France, Germany, Britain and Japan have all fought with Russia and have experienced the way in which its people mobilized for the cause of the motherland, despite the country's lack of democracy.

The role of the state should also be mentioned. Unlike in the West, where the organization of society has conditioned the state system, in Russia the all-powerful state itself has influenced to large extent the workings of society and public and social organizations and institutions. Under conditions of non-democracy, the state's approval was needed for this. What is therefore critically important is that the state actually took a leading role in creating and developing an industrial culture among the Russian population.

It had to do so at times when Russia's technological backwardness – as a frequent result of its social isolation and poor economic infrastructure alike – became patently obvious. As in the time of Peter I. As also in the time of Mikhail Gorbachov, when the ability of the ailing, planned Soviet economy to simultaneously provide welfare, prosperity and defence began to fade.

At other times, there was long tolerance of a non- or even anti-capitalistic stance. There were no recognizable medieval shops, no cartels based on guilds. The comparative lack of trading activity and commercial experience among the broad mass of the population meant that industrial culture in early nineteenth-century Russia developed in an environment where non-industrial traditions prevailed and under conditions of industrial ignorance and serfdom. There was no concerted industrial revolution in Russia; no widespread and well-skilled industrial proletariat; no entrenched commercial infrastructure. By the time the Communist Revolution took place, the broad mass of the Russian people were still agriculturally employed and still far from being consumption-orientated. Until very recently this has still been the case.

Factors in the development of Russian shopfloor attitudes

By 1804 there were in Russia only 2433 factories and mills with a total number of 92 000 workers. By 1893 4.7 per cent of the adult male population of Russia worked in factories, mills and railways.[1]

It was this increase in the demand for workers and the results of the breakdown of the serfdom system in 1861 which virtually forced the creation of labour legislation. The first labour law concerning workers' employment appeared in 1886. Up to then the labour market had not been regulated. The government decided to approve the contractual system, although with many constraints. The employer was obliged to make an individual contract with the employee where such points as conditions of employment, the terms of wages and salary payments were fixed. Also, the Law of 1886 emphasized that the wages should be paid in cash and not in the form of products or on credit terms. Compare this with the similar Truck Act which the British had passed in 1831. That was very important, as the owners of the factories and mills had often done both in the past. The Law of 1886 also made provision for the prosecution of leaders of any strikes of workers. This provided a double support for factory owners since there was a total absence at the time of any workers' associations or trade unions.

In spite of the fact that this law actually recognized workers' rights, it did not make for a level of power equality between employer and employee. A creation of its time and place, it had certain features of a restrictive police-administrative approach which put workers into an even greater economic dependence on the owners of their workplace. This was achieved by ensuring that each worker carried with him or her a total record of employment history. Later, Soviet governments did not change the system. They simply retitled the records as a worker's 'Labour Book' in the Labour Code adopted in 1918. It existed in the same form right up to the third Labour Code of 1971.

It is worth emphasizing that the majority of the Russian population during the period of industrialization in the latter part of the nineteenth century were peasants. For those who left the land for the factory, their workplaces became technical schools. For some, it was where they learnt to read and write. The first owners of the factories also received an education for virtually the first time – in industrial management. Those who were foreigners, setting up in business in Russia, certainly brought with them their own national models – German and French especially – but these had to be adapted to Russian circumstances. Among the key difficulties all faced were the lack of a trained labour force or even just commercially-minded workers for their plants. Factory owners campaigned for (and won) the legal right to retain workers they themselves had trained. To maintain order, harsh discipline was applied. These conditions were those of the early Victorian England of Charles Dickens' novels. Marx drew on such conditions in his analysis of capital–labour relationships to illustrate the political powerlessness of the proletariat at the time.

Human resource management appeared in the former USSR as a system which used the ideas of Frederick Taylor and was based on Taylor's vision of managing people. In 1912–1913 in Petrograd some enterprises applied Taylor's system, but the universal focus was more on the technical side of his approach rather than that associated with the better management of people as a human resource. A strongly negative reaction came from the shopfloor workers and their nascent trade union organizations, which were still weak but growing in number at that time. Nevertheless, Taylor's ideas spread widely among technical managers and wage levels were structured in 1917 in the light of factory production on Taylorist lines. The widespread inference drawn by the popular media from these new ways of working was that labour in Russia was now, as in the United States, organized on a 'scientific' basis.[2]

Taylor's ideas facilitated greatly the creation of infrastructural labour management systems in Russia and, later in the 1920s under the Communist regime, influenced the 'human' resource management system which was implemented under government control at state enterprises. It was during this period that the Russian Central Council of Trade Unions established a Research Labour Institute to study the labour system with a view to improving productivity. Again a technical rather than a human relations orientation was evident. The system developed by the Institute in the 1920s and 1930s was later used as a nationwide model in labour management policy.

It is important to note that Taylor's technical ideas, especially his recommendations on work standarization and output measures, were incorporated into this model. The experience of such institutions with long management traditions in Russia, such as the army and the Church, was also considered as significant by designers of this system. The army had a strong and well-structured organization. It worked well by achieving discipline. The Church was famous for its approach to commanding obedience.

On the other hand, the system was not entirely dehumanizing. While its major concern was with the problems of ordering the human psychology to accept mass, mechanized production in relatively poor, demotivating working conditions, it compensated for this (in the view of the system's promoters at least) by making the worker not just an employee but a 'manager' of the enterprise. This was achieved through the setting up of workers' councils and other sounding boards which actually (or purportedly) represented employees' views to the owners of the enterprise (the state) and to the party hierarchy.

The reforms of industrial management outlined in the Law on the State Enterprise and carried out at the start of the 1990s still heavily endorsed this concept of worker participation. For example, this Law stipulated that 'soviets' of workers at factory level have specific management duties, one of which is to appoint the chief executive, subject to overall control by meetings (*sobranie*) of all the factory personnel. Such an arrangement goes substantially beyond the level of worker participation provided for in the French *conseil d'administration* or in the German *Aufsichtsrat*.

In spite of the priority given to the concept of 'management by the collective of the workers', it was abundantly clear to all concerned that the owner of a factory was the state and that each enterprise was subject to tight jurisdiction not only from the ministry but also the Communist party to whom each factory was bound to pay a sort of tithe (*otchisleniya*). The centralist management of the economy through a state planning and distribution system meant that, when fast and intensive industrialization was called for, a massive level of discipline needed to be imposed to achieve results. In other words, worker autonomy was theoretical.

Part of the reason for external pressure at this level was the relatively low levels of education and implicit productivity of the Russian working population. Workers had had no tradition of any other way of working and Communism did not provide an alternative. Another factor was that there was no spur to change in the form of pressure from shareholders for a better profit performance, since meeting output targets and not return on shareholder equity was the determining factor. As a result, the methods of training and working conditions were not only severe but also remained unreformed.

Under the approach to labour management generally in use since the 1930s, performance indicators were different for workers and managers (so-called soviet administrators). The nature of their employment contracts was different, too. The worker was seen to be the industrialized machine operator and was subject, especially in the period 1930–1960, to a very harsh regime. Management work was, in contrast, labour-intensive and less subject to quantitative controls. In both cases the comparative lack of capital investment in labour-saving equipment meant low levels of productivity.

Output levels (standards) were set by the state. They were based on the output levels which it was considered the best worker could achieve and were specifically aligned with the government's optimum production plans. Occasionally there were even campaigns in particular plants for large-scale teams of workers to carry out very hard and intensive work on particular construction projects (e.g. hydroelectric dams) without compensation. Mass media propaganda in the 1930s played up the need for output and productivity and called for tolerance and understanding of the very low wages that were paid. The aim was to lower worker expectations. It also must be mentioned that by the 1930s the last labour exchange had been closed down and each labour force was attached to its factory.

Such a dependable, cheap and intensive labour supply has been the goal of all governments – Soviet and Russian – ever since. The Taylorist approach to labour and work management, softened (if that is the right word) by elastic concepts of worker self-management, has become deeply embedded in the typical manager's mentality.

As far as worker qualifications are concerned, a new system was set up in the 1930s. This bypassed the earlier division of labour based on integrated job skills or professionalism. Henceforth, the worker's qualifications (and relative status) were determined by the tools and machines he or she was trained to operate or by the technical methods used. Qualification parameters were developed for different workers and wage systems and training procedures became directly linked with these parameters, with training being administered centrally by all-union ministries for each branch of industry.

The government's forecasting and planning of labour demand/supply patterns was conducted quantitatively on the basis of the qualification parameters and the orders placed on businesses via the governments' macro production plans. Little (if any) reference was made to the quality of output except in strategic industries (e.g. defence), where production capability and product were of the essence. As far as consumer product industries were concerned, the consumer was not seen as the determining factor. The accent was firmly placed on the extent to which consumption goods actually pre-empted allocation of relatively scarce resources from other more desirable uses and not, as in the West, on the consumer's interests.

This sort of approach did not/does not now make for entrepreneurship on the part of the typical manager. 'Passive bystanding' might be a more approriate (and critical) term to describe the posture occupied by many so-called 'managers' in the workflow. However, the need to ensure the continued supply of raw materials/parts to the factory in times of scarcity and such elements as manipulating the system to gain access to hard currency have built up in many managers of large-scale enterprises a substantial skill in the area of tactical management of the supply function. Typically, they are masters of the deviant systems that have come into existence to deal with the shortcomings of the state planning system. Such a competence profile is different from that of Western managers and has required a particularly high level of employee-management expertise actually to make good some of the system's worst defects.

Ingenious personnel-handling skills have also been strongly developed in some managers as a result of systemic difficulties in the areas of (1) meeting compulsory production plans with scarce, even inadequate, resources, (2) personal behaviour to ensure maximum staff morale and commitment, (3) counteracting the official notion that incentives and payment-by-results schemes were alien to Soviet (i.e. Communist) value systems by rewarding workers for their output rather than simply for their loyalty to senior management and (4) making up for the defects in the extraordinarily rigid hierachical management structures which permeated Soviet factories and which still endure, a cause of much passivity and not a little alienation. All of these have been acquired in the face of pressure to systematize, indeed dehumanize, the human input to industry.

Managers in the system are, notwithstanding, still characterized by rather low levels of authority and a need to refer things upwards so as to limit risk. There is still a widespread system of 'management by reports' rather than 'management by results'. There is still a culture when management titles do not necessarily connote management capability or even decision-making discretion. Also, it must be said, management knowledge of the requirements for the sound operation of a market economy and the achievement of company competitiveness in a newly created marketplace is still embryonic. Worse, there is still no system for motivating people to work realistically, nor any barriers to the shifting of blame.

Perhaps this is not surprising. After all, the number of managers of central planning bodies in Russia increased sixteen times over the period from 1913 to 1921. Also, although during implementation of the New Economic Policy in the 1920s (to avoid a breakdown of the Soviet economy) the number of state officials was cut down ten times, it increased virtually non-stop once administrative management principles were approved in 1927. Only at the end of the 1980s was action taken to dismantle the all-union ministries which lay at the very centre of the entire edifice of the country's overblown management bureaucracy.

The path ahead

The strong pro-reform vote in the Russian referendum held in April 1993 gives a green light for further real *perestroika* in the Russian polity and economy. It is hoped that this reform will be more structured and effective than that which occurred in the Gorbachev era, although that represented a watershed (*perelom*) in the previous system.

There is much to do in creating a new system of work which will employ and reward those millions of workers whose interests, as employees and consumers, have been so poorly served in the past. Critical to success is the creation of products of which the Russian worker can be proud and which will sell in the new and mighty marketplace that can be created in Russia.

How much that must be done is shown by a poll recently held by the Russian Centre for Research on Social and Economic Issues. A total of 3014 respondents were interviewed in 51 cities of the former USSR. The results were that 50 per cent were satisfied with the job they had, 15 per cent were unsatisfied; no less than 35 per cent made no answer.[3] When people were asked what job they would like to have, most of them pointed quite simply to 'a well-paid job'. Prestige was rated as less important than wage level.

The results of the research by the Centre of Informational Sociology in Kharkov in 1990–1991 revealed similarly discouraging results. The workers inclined to work creatively was the small minority with the highest qualifications. Those who work intensively represented only 6 per cent. No less than 67 per cent said they worked without any interest in the job.[4]

Critical to economic success will be the extent to which the reward system is consistent with improved job performance and the way in which it moves peoples' expectations away from the belief that the average industrial wage is a fair one, irrespective of employment sector. For it is the case that the equality brought about in the years of Communism in wage and salary payments actually reduced labour motivation and diminished the acceptance by the ordinary worker of any responsibility to meet proper standards of production quality. A specific type of worker has come into existence who is oriented to work with the lowest productivity possible and is not interested in the job to be done: the minimalist. Up to now even an attitude of risk-aversion has not been in evidence among workers since their jobs were heavily protected by the system.

One reason for this is anomie – the sense of alienation that comes from subjection to a system that is aimed at making people into machines. Another could well be a deeply felt need to protect full employment by keeping productivity low, even at the cost of low wages. Clearly, the structure of labour values needs to be transformed, just as the production orientation of firms needs to be changed. Work needs to be revalued on the basis of economic contribution rather than some sort of societal approval. Over time the government's approach to guaranteeing full employment will also have to change, just as the development of materialistic behaviour will have to be encouraged. The proper positioning of worker protection and participation has to be worked out in this reform process. These are massive political and philosophical changes which fly in the face of 70 years of Communist history.

Individual managers will have to change their value systems, too, as they are forced to accept new 'rules of the game' – like performance-related pay, unemployment and retraining. Evidence shows that many will welcome the opportunity. For example, one significant factor which has began to make its mark is the desire to set up one's own company. According to one of the recent sociological polls,[5] the picture of the motives and interests of Russian managers in the face of future job reform was the following: 47 per cent consider their existing job to be important; 18 per cent of managers look forward to the possibility of really managing the staff; 12 per cent expect their salaries to increase with the new working conditions and 20 per cent of the managers believe that their work in future will allow them to prove their organizational capabilities. No less than 37 per cent of managers questioned said that they were attracted by the idea of working independently.

Other polls give grounds for optimism. In 1990 a survey was carried out among 119 managers from large cities of the former USSR.[5] Three values were tested in depth: attitude to decision making, optimism in the future and preparedness to accept personal responsibility for results. The managers were directors, top technicians and middle- and low-level administrators. Independence in decision making was a 'must' for mainly top-level managers. They were excited by the entrepreneurial potential involved in such things as designing and carrying out investment policy, and determining by themselves the quality of the products to be made and marketed. They saw their salaries and bonuses as being dependent, in the future, on their contribution.

Most, however, exhibited a degree of concern about their perceived lack of competence in managing people. This, again, is not surprising given the technocratic thrust of the inherited management system, which now clearly needs to be 'repersonalized'. The existing low morale and inadequate business thinking need changing. A massive retraining/business education programme needs to be undertaken. This will concern itself with literally all aspects of the workings of enterprise. Issues in the human resources field that need to be particularly addressed are basic organizational problems in the division of work and the nature/distribution of management authority; coordination and control; motivation; and, as we have seen, performance-related reward systems. The implications for Russia's technically orientated (but, of its type, very high quality) and centrally controlled education system are enormous. So are those for the remnants of its inherited political ideology.[6]

Conclusions

Many of the problems we have outlined result from the human resource management consequences of the Communist centralized planning system as applied to industrial development in the USSR. This took no account of consumer interest, some small account (comparatively) of product quality and total account of quantitative indicators of supply. Negligible attention was paid to the dynamics of human resource management which, in the West, has paid such dividends in terms of worker commitment and productivity. Crude measures were used to deal with all aspects of labour demand/supply management, especially in the 1960s, when the demand for labour was increasing rapidly due to the pace of Russia's heavy industrialization programme. At this time companies were in fact deliberately hoarding their labour resources to ensure no instability in their supply.

Perhaps even more important was the significance of the victory of the Communist Party in the 1917 Revolution and its official endorsement of the Labour Theory of Value. This holds that the worker alone, through his or her labour, creates value in a product and that an additional margin of profit to reward the interests of the private owners of capital represents a sort of theft of the worker's property.

More specifically, however, Taylorism and worker apathy, the government's maintenance of full employment and its insensitivity to labour economics together did not, and do not, create a method for increasing industrial productivity. Bureaucracy abounded so much that the title 'manager' was devalued to the point of loss of meaning. Nor did it make any sense for the salary of the high-ranking technical expert to be the same as for the office clerk.

However, we are now in a 'brave new world'. Positive developments in the organizational culture of some enterprises had been taking place even before *perestroika*, although rather slowly. Now the trends are bound to accelerate and the effects will spread. It is felt that resistance affecting work habits, labour–management traditions and the authority/power of management will break down, and in some fields, quite quickly.

Let us take as an example of change the system of management at the Kaluzhski plant, a major Soviet manufacturer of turbines. In the 1970s it had already started to develop and implement a team system of labour organization. It was not alone, but it was a pioneer in this. The goal was to achieve stable growth by means of relating the incomes of workers to their productivity and using other motivating factors such as workers' participation in enterprise management in a realistic, as opposed to token, fashion.

The workers were divided, within product divisions, into teams which had, so far as could be achieved, individual profit or value-added responsibility. This was completely different from the traditional factory organizational structure of department, brigade and section which typically lacked a formal performance accounting system, at least so far as any concept of profit was concerned. In Khaluzhski, team pay was volume- and quality-related and the performance criteria were increasingly uprated with time. Technical management requirements were, however, satisfied by the way pay was distributed among team members. The method involved a so-called 'labour contribution coefficient' which could be decreased or increased, depending on such factors as labour productivity, output quality, etc.

The increase in earnings achieved through productivity growth in the 1970s and 1980s was partly paid into a productivity scheme (*fond materialnovo po-oschreniya*). This was one of the many financial reserves established within the Soviet factory accounting system, into which surpluses could be paid. Another example is the social fund out of which social spending by the firm – on housing, crêches, hospitals and holiday homes – was made (*fond sotsialnovo razvitiya*).[7] In this instance 70 per cent of the extra money went to the the workers and 30 per cent to the technicians. Separate Team Councils were formed to represent the interests and rights of workers.

The implementation of the new system of labour organization resulted in a high level of annual productivity growth for the plant and increasing stability of employment for its workforce over the period until the late 1980s. But it should be noted that that the Kaluzhski council of teams' councils has actually voted against any privatization of the company.

The environment of the transitional Russian economy will force further change upon such enterprises. One of the spin-off problems that many firms have never previously experienced is going to be worker and manager turnover. For many managers this will be as much of a culture shock as unemployment.[8] A real-time *perestroika* in human resource management for all concerned lies ahead.

It seems that the major skills that Russian managers need to master in order to survive and perform successfully under transitional circumstances are legion. But given some degree of longer-term stability in the legislative framework for business and real growth prospects for the economy, it is quite possible to foresee a much brighter future for the highly-educated but technically-oriented Russian manager than the dismal past of his or her Soviet counterpart.

References

1 Tugan-Baranovski, M., *Russian Factory in the Past and Present – A Historical-Economic Investigation*, St Petersburg, 1898.
2 Gastev, A., *Our Objectives*, Moscow, 1921.
3 Kosmarki, V., 'Two polls of population on motives of labour activity', *Issues of Economics*, No. 1, 1991.
4 *Spiritual Production and Renovation of Socialism*, Kharkov, 1990.
5 Onofrijchuk, A., 'The administrative-command system and motives for managerial activity', *Philosophical & Sociological Thought*, No. 8, Kiev, 1989.
6 McCarthy, D. and Puffer, S., 'Perestroika at the plant level', *Columbia Journal of World Business*, **27**, No. 1, Spring 1992.
7 *Perestroika in the Management of the Firm*, Ekonomika, Moscow, 1989. See also Razumov, A., Sidorova, Zh. and Noskova, S., *The Make-up of Workers' Incomes*.
8 Kochetov, A., 'Hidden unemployment among specialists', *Sociological Research*, No. 5, 1992.

8 Managing people in Spain
Angel Diaz and Paddy Miller

Historical background

In order to understand Spain's history and economic development one has to take into account the profound differences among its geographic regions. These extend way beyond simple regional variations and into language, culture and income differences – some of which originated centuries ago. These historic differences have brought together a nation with very different cultures and a very different understanding of what work is and how to manage people. These differences have to be considered when undertaking any project in Spain.

Under the Catholic kings at the end of the Middle Ages, Spain was immersed in a process of unification and economic change. The unification of Castille and Aragon was the starting point of the modern Spanish state. The all-powerful Church followed the theme of 'Spanish, Reformed and Unique'. As a result the Jews and the Muslims were expelled from the country at the end of the fifteenth century. The attempts by the Spanish crown to mastermind a vast colonial empire were frustrated by competition from more commercially-minded and less feudalistic enemies, and not only the English and the Dutch.

The Bourgeoisie Revolution began under Charles III in the eighteenth century. The aristocracy lost more power and the bourgeoisie (liberal professions such as doctors, lawyers and university graduates) gained both power and political influence. But the gap between the rich and the poor widened, in fact, to an even greater extent than before. The Bourgeoisie later increased their influence through a series of alliances with the monarchy. The latter's power was, in turn, much buttressed by its interdependence on the authority of the Church, just as the Church's authority was itself supported by that of the Crown.

The first half of the eighteenth century was characterized by a protectionist policy while the second half encouraged a more liberal attitude in favour of private commercial interests. Even so, in the agricultural sector, 70 per cent of the land was still held by the Church and the aristocrats and ordinary people had no rights to buy land. In industry, guilds were assumed by the Church to have the role not only of creating wealth through production but also of providing employment. This they did, but without widening patterns of capital ownership and without any income redistribution. Industry was characterized by textiles, shipbuilding, tobacco and sugar, and mining (iron and lead).

The liberalizing effects of trade with the West Indies in the late eighteenth century came increasingly as a shock to the world of commerce, which was forced into a process of economic readjustment. Politics also underwent change. In 1810–1814, in conjunction with the Cortes (parliament) de Cadiz, a profound restructuring of rural life was carried out. Politically, the king became subordinated to parliament, provincial administration and ministries were created, the right of equality adopted and a free market for products was established, with price competition permitted. Nonetheless, the major political impact of this was still limited to the minority groups touched by liberalism (the army, intellectuals and businessmen). The ordinary individual was still without voice and resources.

At the end of the nineteenth century two social groups were clearly demarcated; the bourgeoisie and the uncultured poor. The latter waited in vain for education, social legislation or other privileges already widespread in other more socially developed European countries.

While Spain has had a rich colonial background, the twentieth century has been no less eventful than the distant past. The political turmoil of the post-First World War era gave rise to a bloody civil war between 1936 and 1939. Franco's victory was to lead to the creation of closer ties between Church and state, suppression of all opposition, restriction of trade union activity and the driving into exile of an important group of intellectuals and artists. Business interests were given special attention through the establishment of trade barriers and tariffs. This, in turn, created a closed economy in which Spanish management and labour accepted low productivity and inefficiency as the norm. The framework laid down by Franco was rigidly authoritarian and centralized.

With Franco's dictatorship and the general depression caused mainly by post-civil war conditions, plans were implemented to attempt to revitalize the country, principally the 1957 Stabilization Plan. Its aims were to increase savings, decrease inflation and increase productivity. A second Development Plan, produced in 1964, resulted in a rapid increase in the average standard of living. Many Spaniards began to have access to cars, televisions and home ownership for the first time. This led to the creation of an embryonic new middle class and a migration of people from the countryside to the cities in search of work and a better life.

After the death of General Franco in 1975, the re-establishment of the monarchy and democracy were the first steps in Spain's return to the ranks of the free Western world. The head of state is the king. There is a parliament and Senate, both elected every 4 years. The government is led by the President of the Government, in effect, the prime minister.

Spain is now divided into seventeen autonomous regions which enjoy, under the Democratic Constitution of 1978, different degrees of autonomy. Some, like Catalonia and the Basque Country, have wide discretionary powers regarding education, the civil service, legislation and public care services. They have also begun to promote themselves externally – a fact which is changing the perception of Spain abroad. Others are more closely dependent on the central government in Madrid.

The first phase of democratization was traumatic, as trade unions and political parties proliferated. Not only was the 'vertical syndicalism' of the Franco era (everyone in work had to belong to union dealing with his or her particular industry) replaced by a free trade union structure, but the system substituted control from the Minister for Syndical Relations with full-scale political pluralism.

Strikes for more pay and better conditions were the order of the day and union demands were quickly met. Large industry still had great government involvement and management and government were often synonymous. This situation culminated in the PSOE (Socialist Party) coming to power with the help of the UGT in 1982. Felipe González was its young leader. Spain entered upon a new era as Spanish integration within the European Community became a reality in 1986.

Spain is now still changing fast in many ways and the challenge is to balance its economic activity and social interest. A high rate of direct foreign investment in the past few years, the growing internalization of activity and investment by Spanish companies around the world, and the development of strategic national sectors of activity have added to the complexity of the challenge.

Finally, Spain has tried to change its image worldwide and events like the Expo of Seville, the Olympic Games in Barcelona and the European City of Culture festival in Madrid, all in 1992, have helped to do that. The failure to land the Euro Disney contract mainly through what critics asserted was the lack of strategic vision and alleged mismanagement by the Spanish government show that not everything has been successfully achieved.

Present political and economic system: main features

It is impossible to review issues of workers' rights and the state of trade unionism in Spain without having an insight into two matters of key concern: first, public ownership of industry in Spain and second, the extent of workplace politics in Spanish industry. Both are in a sense paradoxical, since by far the vast majority of Spanish businesses are of small and medium sizes (*Pequenas y Medias Empresas*, or PYMES) and they are heavily under-unionized (see Table 8.1). Yet it is impossible to argue that the legacy of Franco – corporatist relationship between state, large-scale industry, the

Table 8.1 *Stoppages – working days lost*

EU country	% of workforce in union	No. of employees involved in stoppages ('000)					Working days lost per 1000 employees				
		1987	1988	1989	1990	1991	1987	1988	1989	1990	1991
Spain	16.0	2022	7244	1448	776	1896	692	1509	454	265	463
France	12.0	360	403	298	278	408	100	109	179	69	49
Italy	39.6	4273	2712	4452	1664	2951	316	224	300	341	195
Germany	33.8	155	33	44	257	208	1	2	4	15	6
UK	41.5	887	790	727	290	176	164	166	182	83	34

financial sector and the trade union system – has not endured. The larger the industry as an employer of labour (e.g. steel or shipbuilding) or the more prominent the state enterprise, like the giant National Institute for Industry holding company, the more likely it is to be involved in a corporatist power-sharing balance. In the large industry sector the government, the Employer's Confederation (*Confederacion Espanola de Organizaciones Empresaliales*), the trade unions (like the *Union General de Trabajadores* and the Communist *Comissiones Obreras*) are locked together in an industrial strategy route-march which sometimes favours policies of conciliation and consensus – as in the Economic-Social Accord which ended in 1986. Sometimes, however, it results in disputes like the general strike, which took place on 14 December 1988. The industrial members of this coalition are substantial: the state-owned Telefonica, Endesa and Repsol groups, for instance.

As in France, the Spanish government is heavily concerned with the redistribution – as well as the creation – of industrial wealth. Similarly, it works within a 5-year indicative planning framework. The role of the government as a corrector of regional economic imbalances is marked. This is seen as politically necessary in view of the continued salience of agriculture as an employer in Spain and its productivity weakness. The output per capita problem is associated especially with the existence of *minifundios* (small plots) in north-western Spain and the lack of capital intensity on the land.

Workers' rights

Spain is a strong supporter of the European Social Chapter. There is the basic right to unionize and to strike. A strike may be called by the workers' representatives or by the trade union represented in the workplace or by the workers themselves.

In a firm where there are over fifty employees the law requires that a workers' committee has to be formed. A certain minimum number of committee members is elected. This group in turn elects a president and administrative assistant and also formulates its *modus operandi*. Committee members have a 4-year mandate. In smaller companies with under fifty workers similar workers' representatives are elected in proportion to the number of workers. It averages out at one per ten workers.

The committee must meet regularly and, when a special meeting is called, decisions are made by majority vote. If there is a union presence in the firm, its representatives automatically have access to the same information as the works committee, namely, a full shareholders' report prepared quarterly on the sector in which they are employed, full sales and production figures, and employment strategies. These can be printed and distributed to the workers together with details of proposed changes in the structure of the firm, time cuts, job-evaluation studies, installation of new or revision of old systems, job classification, flexitime and shift work, and so on.

They also receive 3 months' advance notification of new employment contracts or extension of existing ones as well as absentee statistics and details of on-the-job accidents. They have the right to collective bargaining and have to be informed of all disciplinary sanctions against workers. They in turn have the right to represent workers in disciplinary matters and committee members are protected from retrenchment, job loss or sanctions. They have total freedom of speech and information on matters concerning work and related issues. Pay is not deducted for hours spent in performing their duties and allowances are usually increased in proportion to the numbers of workers represented. Employment legislation which protects the worker is contained in the Workers' Statutes as well as the Constitution and the Civil Code. EU legislation is also in force in Spain.

A strike committee to deal with any strike negotiations, as well as security during the strike, must be elected by the workers affected by the strike. Five days prior to the strike the employer must be notified of the reasons for the strike and possible measures that could be taken to avoid it as well as details of those on the strike committee. During the strike the worker has no right to remuneration but does retain all rights to social security and state health insurance. Details of comparative approaches to strikes are given in Table 8.2. In 1991 there were around 1500 strikes in which more than 1 900 000 workers participated and 4 421 000 workdays were lost.

Unions

Since May 1977 with the passing of the Trade Union Association Bill the union movement has been dominated by the Union General de Trabajadores (UGT), which is the Socialist general workers union, and the Comissiones Obreras (CCOO) which is the Communist Workers Commission. Both

Table 8.2 *Dealing with strikes*

Element	Is action legal?		Is action legally recognized?		Is there compulsory binding arbitration?		Is there compulsory binding mediation?	
	YES	NO	YES	NO	YES	NO	YES	NO
Official industrial strikes			S,F,I,G	B				
Wildcat unofficial strikes	S,F,I	G,B						
Political protest strikes	I	S,F,G,B						
Disruptive working action	G	S,F,B			I			
Staff lock-out	F#, I,G,B	S[a]						
Peace obligations							S,F,I,B	S,F,I,G,B

[a] Under limited circumstances.
S = Spain, F = France, I = Italy, G = Germany, B = United Kingdom.
Source: The European 21–24 October 1993.

Table 8.3 *Relative militancy league table (1982–1992)*

Element (1982–1992)	Relative EU country rankings				
	Spain	Italy	France	Germany	Britain
No. of strikes	1	3	2	4	5
No. of workers involved in strikes	2	1	3	4	5
Production days lost in strikes	1	2	3	5	4

Source: The European 21–24 October 1993.

retain links with international trade union organizations. Other workers belong to smaller unions. There are also some regional trade unions, for example ELA-STV and LAB in the Basque Country, INGT and CXGT in Galicia and SOC in Catalunia.

Although only 10 per cent of the working-age population are members of the unions, they are fully recognized legally. They are, however, relatively weak as organizational structures and they have been in a slow state of decline for the last five years, despite the Socialist government's passing of legislation favouring the unions and aimed at increasing their power.

The pressure of the unions caused industrial wages to rise swiftly in the final years of the 1980s but with current high unemployment (not helped by high labour costs) the Socialist government has slowly distanced itself from the unions. However, the unions continue to have substantial power to mobilize workers in Spain, as demonstrated in the general strike of 1988 (see Table 8.3).

Negotiating

Negotiations between companies (private or public) and the workers is usually the most controversial aspect of industrial relations. Relations between a company and the union are usually covered by collective bargaining, which group together workers in a certain sector generally at regional or national level. The conditions of employment which they obtain from their respective employers relate to salary increases, fringe and retirement benefits, etc. These collective bargains are usually negotiated between representatives of the unions and the different company sectors at a regional or national level and cover a period of usually one or two years.

The negotiations are usually complicated, although there are few sectors that do not reach a more or less reasonable agreement. The public sector has special problems in obtaining the agreement of the unions to the collective bargains applying to their companies.

In general, one can say that the attitude of the Spanish unions does not correspond to that of most European unions at the end of the twentieth century. Frequently their approach is heavily demagogic and does not bring realistic solutions to the company's problems. Blinded by 'the needs of the workers', they neither see how the market and the competitive international environment (of which Spain now forms part) is evolving, nor that they have to adapt themselves. In many ways the attitudes of the union leaders seems to be reminiscent of an urge to regain some of the dynamism that was lost when the socialist groupings were defeated by civil war. In this sense, and put in relatively crude terms, there is still very often the 'us against them' attitude, the idea of the necessary and inevitable confrontation between companies (rich business executives) and workers (poor and exploited).

Full employment

Comparing the changes in the actively employed population during the last ten years, one can see a loss of employment in agriculture and an increase in the area of services. In the industrial sector, the percentage employment has remained practically the same. Looking at the employed population, the trends are the same. It should be added, however, that the unemployed population (active minus employed) represents a high percentage which has grown moderately in this time, moving for 15.9 per cent to 16.3 per cent (see Table 8.4).

It should be noted that only 1.5 million of the 2.35 million unemployed in 1990 received unemployment benefits. In 1991 the figure was 1.6 million (see Table 8.5). In the first six months of 1993, the number of unemployed

Table 8.4 *Pattern of employment in Spain 1960–1991*

Sector	Active(%) 1960	Active 1982	Employed 1982	Active 1991	Employed 1991	Active(%) 1991
Agriculture	30.70	2165	2061	1541	1345	10.10
Industry	22.30	3216	2824	3218	2892	21.20
Construction	6.30	1323	959	1521	1274	10.00
Services	27.00	5777	5360	7895	7180	52.20
Others	13.70	866	27	984	18	6.50
Total	100.00	13347	11231	15159	12709	100.00

Source: Anvario Estadistico de España, 1992. Inst. Nacional de Estadistica, Madrid (adjusted figures).

Table 8.5 *Average Spanish unemployment 1982–1991 ('000s)*

1982	1872
1983	2207
1984	2475
1985	2642
1986	2758
1987	2924
1988	2858
1989	2550
1990	2350
1991	2289

Source: Spanish government-statistics.

surpassed 3 million, and although the months of July and August indicated some recovery, they were still sufficient to cause alarm.

Corporate ownership and governance

The base of company ownership is the plethora of founders or second- and third-generation family members who own the small or medium-sized companies which account for 85 per cent of the total number of companies in Spain. The state is hoping to withdraw progressively from ownership of major industries (for example, the car industry, where SEAT was sold to the VAG group of Germany). National utilities such as telecommunications, gas and electricity are under examination for this purpose. The mining industry, which is in decline, remains in state control.

A number of publicly floated companies exist but worker participation by way of share issues is largely undeveloped, as also is share holding by the ordinary private citizen.

Power and authority

Employees' attitudes to the exercise of power and authority is highly paternalistic and reactive. The two camps of 'us and them' will be highlighted again later as will the (to date) relatively slow movement towards enlisting employee respect and support for management decisions through consultation and self-determination. The power distance relationship (to use Hofstede's term) is large, meaning that relationships between managers and subordinates will be formal rather than the more informal ones experienced in, for example, the United States or the UK.

Impact of European thinking

About thirty years ago the first official move was made concerning possible membership of Spain in the EC. In 1970 after much diplomatic wrangling a preferential agreement was agreed upon for Spanish agricultural exports to the EC. This preferential agreement was expanded in July 1977. Finally full membership was confirmed, with effect from 1 January 1986.

Joining the modern, democratic and wealthier EC countries to the north was an enormously important moment for Spain. Spain set great store on its membership of the European Community and at first its sense of enthusiasm was palpable. Almost all Spaniards, along with the President, embraced Europe. It fulfilled economic, political and social needs. The Spanish economy had been accustomed to a protectionist approach and the challenge was to dismantle tariffs and to try to compete with countries with a history of free competition and often superior products. A timetable was set for tariff dismantling and this was completed in January 1993.

The peseta joined the EMS in 1989 within the 6 per cent fluctuation range. Demand growth was well above the EC average and Spanish investment demand increased rapidly. However, since the end of 1992 this picture has changed substantially, both economically and emotionally. The turning point may have been the Danes' 'No' vote to Maastricht (now reversed) which caused a shockwave in Spain. The Spanish felt that in the light of the great changes that their economy had to effect to join the Community as well as the sacrifices they were willing to make in the future they themselves were the ones who had most reason to say 'no' and not the comparatively rich Danes, for whom economic and monetary union was seen as a relatively easy undertaking. However, as one of the poorer states in Europe, Spain benefits handsomely from EU regional development grants (presently between 6 billion and 7 billion pesetas per annum).

Influence of American and Japanese industrial thought

The presence of large operations in Spain run by companies such as General Motors and Hewlett Packard and Nissan, Sanyo and Sony has brought with it new methods and approaches in, for example, production techniques and human resources. The underlying Spanish culture has required considerable adaptation of philosophy and thought, at least in the short term, as new ways of doing things are slowly learned.

Key features in the current state of industry and commerce and their major effects

Industry types

In Franco's time Spain had relied on heavy industries with low productivity and high-cost structures. Many of these industries were obsolete. Spain had no history of research and development. The challenge to industry has been one of updating or conversion, with the implication that there would be a need for the retraining and refocusing of the labour force as well as acceptance of high levels of unemployment.

The car industry is perhaps the single most important manufacturing industry in Spain. Both directly and indirectly, the industry is a substantial employer and is responsible for 10 per cent of the GDP. Plants of SEAT, VW, GM, Nissan, Renault, Suzuki, Ford and IVECO are all around the country, and they produced almost 2 million vehicles in 1992. In summary, most Spanish companies are becoming part of the global activities of major multinational companies in the sector, including the sale of many parts and components producers to foreign companies.

Spain also has a proficient wine industry. Its textile industry consists of mostly single companies that have survived the catastrophic crisis in which much textile manufacturing moved to Asian and North African countries, as a result of comparatively low labour costs outside Spain. There are a number of very specialized high-tech minimills in the steel industry, for example.

Shoe making, and all the industries related to leather, are also well established in Spain and export to foreign markets. Heavy industries, like shipbuilding and steel, once very developed, are now dedicated to niche operations aimed at not competing, in general, in global markets.

In the services sector, the most important area for the country is tourism. It accounts for 12 per cent of GDP, and it generates US$20 billion of annual income for Spain. More than 50 million tourists visit the country each year. Strategic repositioning is taking place with a move to high-quality, multiple-location products that will require the retraining of thousands of people.

Banking is now a highly profitable business in Spain. Modern and very well equipped (software and hardware), the industry has not been held back by outdated working practices. However, savings institutions are battling against venerable, sometimes outdated (with clear exceptions), commercial banks for funds.

Retailing is also a huge sector is Spain, with little Spanish presence and foreign (mainly French) domination, although the largest private company in the country is the Spanish EI Corte Ingles. Other international companies, like Alcampo and Carrefour, are also present.

The construction sector is also well developed and competes in international markets, having some degree of influence in South America and the Arab countries.

Finally, partly government-owned oil and telecommunications companies are among the medium-sized firms (in European terms).

Technology change

Technology change has been rapid in, for example, the motor and retailing industries, where a foreign presence is felt. The increase in investment since 1975 allowed substantial advances to be made in this regard, though Spain still lags behind its EU partners. The thrust is attributed predominantly to foreign influence.

Status of professions

The professions are well respected and the quality of training high. But, in common with other countries, teachers and doctors have lost considerable status; doctors because of oversupply. For example, there are thought to be approximately 20 000 doctors who do not have employment as doctors and are forced to do other types of work. Spanish accountants, lawyers and management consultants have felt the increase in competition from international firms in recent years.

Wages

Minimum wages have evolved steadily in recent years. In 1983 the statutory minimum wage for an 18-year or older worker was 32 160 pesetas (US$240) per month. By 1992 this had risen to 56 280 ptas (US$420) per

Table 8.7 *Age distribution of the population (%)*

	1991	1970
Less than 15 years	27.791	19.37
Between 15 and 45 years	41.13	44.66
Between 45 and 65 years	20.57	21.83
More than 65 years	9.67	13.77
	100.00	100.00

Source: As for Table 8.4.

month. Average earnings per hour were of 1087 pesetas per hour (US$8.11) with variation between 1406 pesetas (US$10.5) for white-collar and 877 (US$6.55) for blue-collar workers, respectively.

Productivity

There has been much debate in Spanish society about workforce productivity and, in recent years, a simultaneous and associated growing decline of employment opportunity and a progressive increase in the productivity of the workforce. The unions are opposed to any increase in productivity that leads to redundancies. The debate recognizes the importance of general and vocational training in achieving productivity increases. The latter is necessary to make redundant workers fit for other work. However, the unions have been known to argue that vocational training programmes are not well suited to their workers' needs.

What is clear is that the Spanish workers' productivity, especially in small and medium-sized businesses, is still far below the productivity levels achieved in countries such as the United States or Japan.

Demographics

According to 1991 official census data, the Spanish population that year was 39.4 million, 51 per cent of which were females. Since 1900 the population has grown by 111 per cent, with a clear difference between rural and urban areas, the growth of the latter being 357 per cent in the same period. Table 8.7 contains relevant 1991 census data.

There has been a substantial improvement in the literacy level of the population since 1960. This may be associated with the considerable fall in agricultural employment (30.7 per cent of total jobs in 1960 as opposed to 10

Table 8.8 *Trade balance (in pesetas)*

1982	−1240
1983	−1330
1984	− 887
1985	−1005
1986	−1139
1987	−1840
1988	−2330
1989	−3262
1990	−3268
1991	−3572

Source: As for Table 8.4.

per cent in 1991) and commensurate rises in the numbers of industrial and services jobs – 10 per cent and 20 per cent rises over this period, respectively.

Natural resources

Spain was once characterized by being extremely wooded. Now only parts of these woods remain but still produce pulpwood (approximately 8 625 000 m^3 per annum) and sawlogs (approximately 4 272 000 m^3 per annum).

Spain has other natural resources. Its coal production, although declining in recent years, still amounts to more than 14 million and 17 million tons of hard coal and brown coal, respectively. In fishing, Spain's total catch in 1988 was 1 430 000 metric tons (live weight), being particularly strong in Atlantic mackerel and cod, sardine, tuna, hake and blue whiting.

Trade balance

Spain has significantly increased its trade balance deficit in the last decade. The year-end balances of the last decade in Table 8.8 show the important growth of the trade deficit in the past three years. The ratio between exports and imports was maintained at around an average of 157 per cent in these same years.

According to the tariff registers, Spain is a net importer and exporter of:

- *Exports:* Vegetable products, fats and oils, footwear, stone and cement transport material, arms and munitions.
- *Imports:* Live animals, food, drink and tobacco, petroleum, chemical products and their derivatives, plastics, furs raw and finished, wood,

Table 8.9 *Education data 1989–1990 (students)*

	Schools	Students
Pre-university	39 315	1 000 031
EGB	183 647	5 080 991
BUP and COU	3 019	1 470 816
Professional training	2 260	817 099

Source: Ministry of Education.

paper and raw materials, industrial textiles, pearls, precious stones and metals, common metals, machines and apparatus, optics, photographic material and precision instruments, *objets d'art* and antiques.

Legislative framework for managing people

Education

The education system's last major reform was in 1970. Education at all levels is free and compulsory up to the age of fourteen in public schools. Private schools are an alternative and are attended by about 30 per cent of pupils. Instruction is in Spanish, except in the Basque Country and Catalonia, where the local language is encouraged.

The education structure broadly follows the same pattern as is found in the rest of the EU. Primary education lasts eight years. Some pupils leave school on receipt of the EGB (*Education General Basica*) certificate after primary school but this is not encouraged.

At secondary education level the students have a choice. They can follow the BUP stream which will, after three years and a final year of university preparation (called the COU), allow entry into university. Alternatively, they can undertake the technical training 'FP route' which provides for training in specific industries. The latter is under considerable criticism at present for not preparing trainees adequately for their selected industries. Recent figures are set out in Table 8.9.

University education costs a nominal amount unless one attends the few private universities, where the cost is much higher. The time spent in obtaining a degree is usually five years. The first three years lead to a diploma and the final two to the degree which is equivalent to a masters degree. Subsequently, doctoral studies may be pursued.

At this point a mention of the state of management studies may be appropriate. As at all other levels of education, management education has been traditionally dominated by religious orders. The most prestigious business schools are run by orders such as the Jesuits and Opus Dei. There has been great demand for masters diplomas (especially the MBA) and business schools have thrived, despite there being no official state recognition of the management diploma. At present there are approximately 120 business schools in total, varying from small single-course schools to highly sophisticated schools that compete with the best of schools in Europe. IESE, ESADE, Instituto de Empresa and Deusto are some of the better schools who offer a wide range of programmes. Only IESE provides programmes in English as well as in Spanish.

In order to control the proliferation of business schools and the resulting drop in quality, an association (AEEDE) has been formed to set standards and to guide the public regarding the best courses available. Institutions which belong have to comply with the high standards laid down by the association.

Social security and pensions

Social security payments are compulsory and are deducted from the worker's wage before payment and contributions are also made by the employer. Both groups must contribute to the system according to predetermined levels based on professional grade, sector and other factors.

Social security covers sickness and maternity benefit, unemployment benefit and pension. In order to quality for sickness benefit of any type a medical certificate must be presented to the employer within five days of the accident/sickness occurring.

In the case of common illness or accidents which are not work-related 60 per cent of the statutory base is usually paid and can continue for a period of six years. However, in many cases employers are obliged to pay a full 100 per cent due to prior collective agreements.

Maternity benefits are paid for sixteen weeks or longer if the mother's condition requires it, subject to certain qualification requirements.

The amount of retirement pension to which a worker is entitled is based on the period over which contributions have been made (minimum 15 years, two years in the last eight years of work). Pensions are also available to people who are not eligible for them under the social security system.

The basic retirement age is 65 years with exceptions for certain professions such as miners, sailors, bullfighters, etc., and 55 years is the lower limit. The pension is normally reduced by 8 per cent for each year of early retirement.

The amount of a contributory retirement pension is calculated on certain variables. Partial retirement is possible under certain conditions and when these apply the insured is entitled to 50 per cent of the amount of the pension and the additional salary earned is not exempt from contributions. The number of pensions in the social security system in Spain in 1991 was 6 253 400, with an average pension of 48 000 pesetas per person, which implies an expense of 300 billion pesetas.

Employment and employment conditions

Legislation makes provisions for various types of employment contracts in addition to the ordinary work contract which is for full-time work until retirement. For example, temporary contracts include those which allow a company to renew the contract of a worker for three years. However, at the end of this period the company, if it wishes to continue employing the worker, has to convert it into a fixed contract. Special contracts for part-time work, mature workers, temporary work, job-creation schemes, apprenticeships, employment at home, employment for the physically handicapped as well as a host of others are also available.

When it becomes necessary to discontinue a contract and terminate a worker's services for whatever reason on the part of an employee, the cost is often high and the unions have made it very difficult to dismiss anyone. This is fully in keeping with their collectivist orientation. Except in the case where the worker voluntarily renounces the contract, unemployment benefit is due for a period of two years from the Department of Social Security.

The working week is, by law, set at 40 hours which may be continuous or divided. The working day may not exceed nine hours. Night work is remunerated at 25 per cent above the normal pay rate. Overtime is limited to 80 hours per worker per year and may be remunerated at least 75 per cent above the normal rate of pay or exchanged for time off depending on the individual contract. Workers under the age of eighteen are barred from doing overtime. The weekly rest is calculated as a day and a half, although two has become the norm in most sectors. Annual holidays are set at 30 days per calendar year and 2 months' notice must be given to the employer prior to taking a holiday. Such regulations are strictly adhered to and are in strict contrast to the more liberal approach to work management in the UK.

Health and safety

The legislation is comprehensive and requires appointment of health and safety officers from the workforce for enforcement and information-dissemination purposes. The minimum standards for health and safety are set down in the Orden Ministerial dated 9 March 1971. These apply to all places of work and aim to avoid unnecessary risk to workers. The legislation is extremely detailed and done by industrial sector. Every aspect is covered, ranging from acceptable levels of noise, air toxicity, light, radiation, air temperature and humidity as well as control of the physical environment, including the sizes of staircases, changing and dining rooms, etc. Fire prevention, hygiene, methods of food handling, etc. are covered in detail as well as technical safety measures related to specific activities in specific industries.

In companies of between 100 and 500 workers the employees must choose someone who will be responsible for health and safety in the company and in larger firms of over 100 workers a special committee must be appointed with at least three workers' representatives. Their duty is to see that the relevant health and safety rules are understood and applied. Larger firms must have their own medical assistance available on the premises. All firms are subject to regular inspections and any breaches of the regulations are heavily penalized.

Equal opportunities

The law provides for equal opportunity for all regardless of race, colour, sex or creed. According to the Workers' Statute there can be no discrimination in recruitment or employment on the basis of sex, civil status, social condition, religious or political convictions, union membership on non-union membership, language, etc. This also includes equal treatment of legally employed foreigners. There are fiscal inducements for the employment of the physically handicapped. Women represent about a third of the workforce and there are a number of government training programmes designed to encourage this trend.

Salient features of management practice

Recruitment and selection

The contracting of personnel has evolved a great deal in Spain in the last years. Headhunting companies began to proliferate from 1986. This method is now frequently utilized in the selection process for positions in the company.

It is also more common to use part-time employment agencies to cover certain positions in the firm. 'Executive Rental' companies have appeared which 'lend' the executives that they have on staff as temporary employees of different companies. It must be mentioned that the contracting and selection of personnel is still not well developed in the majority of the small and medium-sized companies.

Firms are becoming more and more conscious of the importance of having a description of the work position and looking for the correct person to cover it. However, it has required much time and effort for this philosophy to be applied to work positions on the production line, whether it be industrial (assembly) or services (restaurants, hotels, etc.).

In the majority of Spanish small and medium-sized companies the personnel department is still more an administrative department than a department for the management of human resources, and has traditionally devoted little attention to the professional development of the individual. This aspect is closely related to the lack of training in the company, which will be discussed later.

In general, it can said that the methods of selection and evaluation of personnel in the Spanish company have improved considerably in the last few years, and the average Spanish business executive is beginning to realize the importance it has in the success of the company.

Training

Training within companies is experiencing a spectacular period of growth. The difference between vocational/professional training and technical training of company management should be noted. The former has always been important and has existed in Spain in different forms. The latter began an important development only at the beginning of the 1980s. Now one can find a vast supply of courses of all types and qualities.

Significant differences exist in the managers' attitudes towards the training of their employees. In the industrial environments of the big cities the manager is conscious of the need for training. However, there are many areas in Spain where managers have not yet understood the necessity or the benefits of quality training and they opt for no training at all or training which does not fit their needs. These areas are highly correlated to the easy success of tourism in the 1970s and 1980s and also to under-development.

Two reasons which constantly appear as excuses for not having extensive employee training programmes are that training is more of an expense than an investment and a lack of confidence in the company's capability to retain the employees once they have been trained. In the case of executives, this changes a little. When speaking of training at the MBA level, the company attempts to protect its investment by linking payment of the MBA programme's fees to the length of time the individual remains with the company after the course.

Employee development, appraisal, career management, and staff planning

Spanish companies have traditionally been weak in the area of employee development and Spain has one of the lowest investments in human resource figures in Europe. As a result, the areas of staff planning and training have lagged behind most European companies. Only recently have efforts turned to increased training especially where government subsidies are offered for on-going training.

The concept of a career within the company, independent of whether one is the owner's son or daughter, has gained recognition in recent times and more and more companies are designing career paths for their employees. These are very much related to the ability to measure the performance of the individual.

Traditionally, in the Spanish company it has not been considered very seemly to relate the remuneration of individuals to their performance in their posts and the fulfilment of objectives except, naturally, in sales departments. This tendency has changed drastically in the last few years and now the Spanish company is concerned above all to discover what methods it can use to increase the performance of its employees, improving the methods of evaluation relating to the fulfilment of objectives in order to achieve this. In this sense, the concepts of evaluation are intimately tied to the development of the employee within the company. The company believes firmly in the fact that the people trained within the company will always be better, on average, than those that come from outside, and that it has to invest time which is very expensive for the latter to familiarize themselves with the company.

One notable factor has an important influence on the criteria of selection and training within Spanish companies. Within the great majority of family companies (more than 90 per cent), almost all of them small or medium sized, the owners are people who have received, on average, very little academic training but a lot of training from their own life experience, which, they are convinced, is better. With the generational change this attitude is gradually changing and their successors are now altering the structures of selection and training within the companies. This progressive professionalisation brings with it a greater capacity to design work posts, to look for a suitable people to fill them and, in order to recruit a good professional, the company can create high expectations of further training and development within the company. In this sense, the *planning* of the human resources within the company has become very important for the proper discharge of this function.

Throughout this chapter it has been indicated that it is not so much that Spanish business executives have omitted to address many of the functions mentioned here but that they have done them in a very informal manner, perhaps poorly organized and without adequate planning. Until recently, the human resource function which has enjoyed success in other countries have been more a drain on other resources than a productive process. This has changed radically in Spain but the business sector requires time and the above-mentioned generational change to be able to implement adequate systems in the companies.

Employment termination and redundancy

The termination of employment in a Spanish company is a complicated and expensive matter. Those employees designated as 'fixed contracts' to whom the company has promised to keep contracted in employment for life are very expensive to dismiss if the decision to do so is unilateral on the part of the company. A statutory indemnity of 45 days' salary for each year worked has to be paid and an indeterminate amount, normally high, in return for which the employee agrees to rescind his or her contract without involving the company in an employment law suit. The same applies to non-continuous fixed contracts which allow employees to work from year to year in areas and sectors that are highly seasonal like tourism but which guarantee the position. Everything considered, the termination of a fixed contract is an onerous matter which retards companies who have been able to adapt their production systems and workforce to the requirements of the market.

It is possible that in 1994 the employment and dismissal of workers will be somewhat liberalized. Without this flexibility, which is opposed by all the unions, Spanish companies cannot see their way out of the present economic crisis.

In the light of these potential developments it is increasingly common for employees to protect their contracts with a clause providing for a high indemnity in the event of dismissal before the termination of the contract.

Apart from dismissal various other forms of redundancy are permitted with similar indemnification requirements. Maternity leave of up to sixteen weeks is permitted as well as complicated allowances for different types of absenteeism for other than health reasons (e.g. in the case of a death in the family).

Pay system

Only a few years ago there was a very rigid salary structure. Now there are a great variety of systems. The variable part of the salaries has increased spectacularly and, at the same time, all types of payment are now possible, from cash to payment by credit cards, travel, cars, etc., depending, obviously, on the level of the employee. Until recently, these types of income were not considered to be such from a fiscal viewpoint. Now they all have to be recognized and taxed as part of the individual's remuneration.

Basing part of a salary on performance is also beginning to be applied to other levels of the company, including the worker. Fixing objectives and working in teams to achieve them is beginning to form part of the company culture.

In the public sector there is a gradual movement, but small companies are still reluctant to change because they do not trust their employees and fear the consequences for the future.

Employment structure

With Spanish unemployment up to 2.5 million people (more than 20 per cent of the workforce) by mid-1993 recruitment should be an area of little concern to management. This is not the case, as there are shortages of specialized skills in certain areas and rigid labour laws that make dismissal difficult and expensive as mentioned earlier. These laws have as their basis the protection of employees rather than the creation of business opportunities.

In recent years less rigid contractual conditions have been introduced for companies wishing to employ people on a temporary or part-time basis. With Spain's cyclical tourist industry this has meant rapid falls in the unemployment statistics during August of each year. Combined with attractive training support programmes within autonomous regions these contracts constitute 40 per cent of all contracts registered with the Instituto Nacional de Empleo (INEM, or National Institute of Employment).

INEM is the centre of all labour recruitment and registration activities as all vacant posts, completed contracts and dismissals have to be registered. Although recruitment by companies follows similar patterns to those adopted in the rest of Europe INEM must be informed of all labour movements. Personnel-placement agencies are very active in the labour market especially at managerial levels. Newspapers in the main centres (*El Pais* in Madrid and *La Vanguardia* in Barcelona, for example) also provide a channel for recruitment efforts.

Ironically, although unemployment levels have been high over the past five years many foreigners have entered the labour market, either taking posts in sectors (e.g. agriculture and construction) that are undesirable for location and/or monetary reasons to the local population or that cannot be filled locally (e.g. management positions). Unless EU citizens, prospective employees must have residence and work permits.

Organizational change

Spanish companies have typically experienced a profound transformation since the beginning of the 1980s. The opening of a free market, entry into the EU, the liberalization of the capital market, the arrival of foreign capital and, in the same international context, ever more competition have obliged Spanish companies to change. They have suffered great difficulties in surviving as they are accustomed to products of intermediate quality which satisfy an unsophisticated demand. Many companies have disappeared and those that have survived have been characterized by a notable desire to fight, increasing the quality of the products and services, and selling them in the outside world. In general, these changes have decidedly influenced the management structure, and have made Spanish managers more flexible in facing a changing environment.

Philosophy, values and culture

Few Spanish companies can be described as having an explicit company culture. While it may be obvious that each company has a way of doing things, it is difficult to find companies of any size which have made the effort to put on paper exactly what they believe they do, how they want to carry it out and their priorities. Generally, the great majority of companies are clearly marked with their founders' personalities and there are few that have reached a professionalization separate from the family owners.

The general belief does exist that employees and their employers should 'play against' each other but this is generally becoming less strongly held. In this sense it must be influenced by the fact, as mentioned earlier, that the industrial base is composed of small and medium-sized companies. Companies are progressively coming around to the idea that, no matter how small, the company *can* know its clients and its market well, sell quality products in the appropriate niche, and train its employees in an appropriate manner.

The employees have experienced an evolution in the same direction. It is increasingly frequent to find company committees who want their workers to learn, diversify their knowledge base, participate in the decisions of the company, etc. However, there is still a long way to go before one can speak of effective communication between directors and workers.

Apart from the works council, there exists little worker participation in the decision-making organs of the company and it appears that it will be some time before this happens. At present, few companies have a workers' representative on the board of directors.

Human resources strategy

In summary, one can conclude that the management of human resources is an area that is still lacking in Spanish companies. It has acquired great importance in recent years but is still far from being a fundamental concern for the majority of Spanish directors. Training forms part of few companies' strategy for growth and improvement but the employee is still seen, sadly, by a large number of Spanish companies as an 'enemy' who has to be controlled.

If one accepts that change is necessary at all levels, then it is the family business in which changes are most necessary. As the majority are small and medium-sized companies, it is these and, above all, the latter which constitute the company base of the country which are critical to achieving widespread change.

It has been identified earlier in this chapter that the human element is the principal motor of activity and success in business, but this change of attitude has still not been achieved at the lowest levels of the company. The motivation and recognition of the production line worker – unlike those in direct contact with the public – is still not a priority for medium-sized Spanish companies. This is changing very rapidly but it will be a process of 'natural selection' in which those who bring about the change will be the survivors.

9 Managing people in the Netherlands

Terry Garrison and Paul Verveen

Introduction

Of all the major European nations dealt with in this book, Holland is by far the smallest. It has a land area of just over 41 000 km² and a population in the region of 15 million. This is not its only claim to fame, however: it is justifiably famous for the tolerance of its people. The approaches of the Dutch government and business to a wide range of human resource issues in industry and commerce have, until recently, been a byword for participative management in the European Union. Equal forebearance has been shown by city authorities throughout Holland to many facets of a changing social culture, as well as to immigration, which produce rather more authoritarian reactions elsewhere in Europe.

Part of the reason for this tolerance is the extraordinarily rich melting-pot of Dutch culture which has instilled into its population an age-old capacity for handling the many significant problems associated with the nation's politico-economic history and its ethnic and religious population mix.

Holland's economic base is especially interesting in this regard. Being predominantly flat and agricultural, parts of the country were – until the construction of the Oosterschelde barrier – at the mercy of the North Sea while elsewhere the ever-present danger of fresh-water flooding meant that the Dutch system of dykes and continuous land drainage was imperative. The Netherlands is a major industrial producer, certainly, but it derives a substantial benefit from its geographical position and its role as an entrepôt economy. Rotterdam is the centre of a giant web of transport routes which span the European continent. Holland derives much advantage from this situation, but only because it has become capable of handling the diversity of challenge which is involved.

John Child, the eminent cross-cultural analyst, has argued[1] that there are three broad schools of thought on the factors which have influenced the background to the way in which people are managed. The first is the 'contingency' school.[2] This sees the level of industrialization reached by a particular country as the key issue. The second – or 'culture' – school concentrates on the extent to which a nation's inherited and newly created social institutions determine human resource management systems. The culture school would, therefore, be concerned with such artefacts as trade unionism, the nature of the electoral system or 'Ivy League' education as salient contextual variables. The third is the 'political philosophy' school.[3] Here the focus is on the form of the ruling political system. Whoever in fact, owns the means of production (state or private) and dictates their pattern of use will also determine the nature of the management approach applied.

As we shall see in this chapter, the Netherlands is an example of a country where researchers from all three sets of schools would find no shortage of material to support their arguments. The concept of a Dutch management culture 'melting pot' is not misplaced, either, when one considers the current problematic issue of de-layering within enterprises.[1] Here, the myriad management challenges involved in moving organizations from a settled and secure hierarchical past into a much more competitive future are keenly felt.

The starting point for our review of the heterogeneous human resources management culture in Holland is the nation's history.

Matters historical

In the sixteenth and seventeenth centuries the Netherlands vied for position with its chief commercial rival, England, as Europe's leading trading nation. Its 'fluitschips' of some 900 tonnes burden were particularly suited to international commerce and, by the year 1650, the Dutch navy was four times that of England's. The Dutch transport capability, together with the decline in Spanish and Portuguese commercial competition (particularly after the defeat of the Spanish Armada in 1588), led to the country's growth as a major colonial power. Batavia in Java was already well established as a key Dutch trading centre by the year 1630.

Things were done on a grand scale by ambitious men in those times. For example, the Dutch East India Company was founded by Grand Pensioner Barneveld in 1602. Out of this grew a commercial empire that was worldwide and extraordinarily rich, as Amsterdam, the former trade capital of the Netherlands, testifies. The company's banker – the Bank of Amsterdam – was established as a state institution with a monopoly of currency exchange and no shortage of investment capital. The Amsterdam bourse also dates from the early seventeenth century. It was a major European share-trading centre, supported by the wealth of Huguenots and Jews who had fled from religious persecution in France and Spain, respectively.

By the end of the eighteenth century, England was taking over from the Netherlands and Spain as the leading colonial power. Aided by its trade links with Russia (which brought in masts from Archangel), England could build larger and more powerful ships, Holland having fewer deep-water slipways than England from which to launch its East Indiamen. Furthermore, England's success in negotiating the Treaty of Utrecht in 1713 gave it the lucrative monopoly of shipping African slaves to French and Spanish colonies in the West Indies and the New World. This helped with England's industrialization – since colonies provided ready-made and well-protected markets – and reinforced its rapidly growing naval superiority. Nevertheless, the continuation of Dutch colonial rule in the Far East maintained the flow of wealth to Holland, to the point where this country was still, in the mid-twentieth century, a world-class colonial power. Just as the admixture of refugees from other parts of Europe had helped to create the Netherlands' commercial base, so also has colonialism given the country a merchanting orientation, a trading sense and a cross-cultural richness which few in the European Union can match.

In a way, Holland inherited commercial leadership from Belgium. Even by the eleventh century, Flanders was renowned throughout Europe for the quality of its wool. From 1300 onwards large and successful fairs operated in Ypres, Bruges, Turnhout and Lille to trade wool for such products as French wine, Italian luxuries and Baltic amber. Bruges, in fact, grew to become the market capital of Europe in this medieval period.

As elsewhere in Catholic Europe at this time, all trade was subject to tight public control through the cartel-like guild corporations, sanctioned by Church and feudal authorities alike. Not only were products to be sold at regulated prices with interest rates strictly controlled ('pretium justum'), but businesses could be punished heavily if they traded outside hours ('pre-vention') and bought in bulk for unlicensed retail sale later ('regratterie'). One especially heinous crime was any attempt to corner the market ('accaparement').[1]

Antwerp rose to success as Europe's leading financial centre as a function of Belgium's commercial success and as a function of that country's medieval relationship with Spain. It was a major port serving the Spanish fleet literally from Columbus's time onwards. In fact its bourse dates from 1485. However, as Spain declined in military importance so, too, did the role of Antwerp. Once William of Orange had driven the Spanish Duke of Alba out of the Netherlands and had become 'stadthouder' (royal protector), Holland was free to develop along its own economic and political path, no longer subject to the hegemony of others.

It is from this past that the Dutch derive a characteristic that needs to be set in contrast with the later colourful colonialist experience. With the Spanish domination came a rigid pattern of religious faith; this was later amplified by Calvinism in the Catholic South. Even when Protestantism gained ascendancy in the North it led to no spontaneous outburst of social liberalism as in England. The good burghers of Amsterdam, as represented in Rembrandt's paintings in the Rijksmuseum, exude solidity, respectability and dourness of temperament, as well as of clothing.

Therefore today there is a form of social schizophrenia in Holland between the old and the new – the ancient towers of Delft, Leiden and Utrecht and the modern port of Rotterdam, for instance – and between the outward-looking colonial trading past and the traditional inward-looking Dutch values. This, in many ways, is the major management problem for the Dutch government as it wrestles with the social problems inherited from a richer past.

The politics of change

Industrialization of the Netherlands occurred relatively late. Belgium had moved ahead in manufacturing terms since it had domestic access to the key factor of production it needed (coal) for the manufacture of steel. Holland, in contrast, after the political break with Belgium in 1831, was a country more heavily dependent on agriculture and commodity trade. However, as Germany grew to industrial hegemony under Bismark, so the Netherlands – Germany's next-door neighbour – moved ahead. The country's social legislation marched in step with Germany's – for example, the legalization of strikes (1872) and the Van Houten law abolishing child labour (1874).

A turning point was experienced in the railways strike of 1903, when it was widely realized that, for such a small country as the Netherlands, future social conflict was to be avoided at all costs. The population was simply too geographically-concentrated and the dangers of political schism arising from external religious or regional squabbling were too great for comfort in such industrial disputes. Henceforth, the trade unions grew in political stature, even if their membership did not grow overly in size. They became, especially after the Second World War, increasingly institutionalized as contributors to the government in terms of socio-industrial legislation.

The key elements of the platform on which human resources management now rests were, in fact, established in the period 1945–1958. It was a time of political domination by the left – perhaps not surprisingly because of the need for industrial and social reconstruction after the war – and many of the infrastructural moves bear the philosophical imprint of the socialist Willem Drees. For example, the universal Labour Scheme (*Plan van de Arbeid*) and the central planning system (*Centraal Planbureau*) have parallels in socialist legislation in Britain. Of particular interest are bodies called Statutory Industrial Organizations (*Publiekrechtelijke Bedrijfsorganisatie*, or PO). These were organizations whose job it was, within each industry sector, to ensure the formation and maintenance of a forum for debate on wages, prices and working conditions. The forum took the form of a council on which were represented management, workforce and the government itself (*kroonleden* or independent advisers to government). The Social and Economic

Council (*Sociaal-economische Raad,* or SER) stood at the apex of this system of deliberative organs and was tasked with reporting to government on the needs of industry.

If we couple this socialist planning approach with the government's continued support at the time for traditional price and market-sharing cartels we have clearly a corporatist approach to industrial management. Of even greater importance to the present situation is the fact that the philosophy of immediate post-war governments was avowedly redistributive. The combination of a governmental thrust to greater wage and income equality, plus Marshall Aid, plus the wage and price restraint delivered by the SER system, plus central planning delivered substantial post-war economic expansion. It was a Dutch golden age.

The exploitation of Holland's offshore gas and oil reserves at Slochteren from 1959 onwards aided industrial expansion considerably. The economy grew and with it an increasing investment in new technology by major firms which had begun first – on the basis of bombed-out factories – in 1946. Productivity rose strongly and with it claims by the unions for higher wages and improved working conditions. The governments of the late 1960s and early 1970s responded to this pressure by strengthening the raft of socialist measures on which the post-war economy had been built. They launched a suite of programmes to increase pensions, allowances and benefits and raised the statutory minimum wage.

The platform was further expanded by the Investment Act (*Wet op de Investeringsregeling*) brought in by Ruud Lubbers, Finance Minister in Den Uyl's government (1973–1977) This was intended to allow the government greater selectivity in making state investments.

During this period the economic policies pursued by successive governments were Keynesian in thrust. Even after the oil crisis in 1973, when it became recognized that oil income had (by permitting high wage increases and expanding the money supply) in fact helped to overheat the economy. Only in the light of the very serious balance of payments crisis in 1982 did a Dutch government start to apply the brakes.

It was Ruud Lubbers himself that led this administration. Because of its tough economic stance it became known as the 'no-nonsense cabinet' or, in terms of a British parallel, 'Conservative'. It was, in fact, a centre–right coalition bent on a programme of state privatization, industry deregulation, monetarism and supply-side changes. Of course, from a social standpoint, the government was still focusing major attention on bringing down unemployment and restoring economic growth as well as containing inflation.

Although this government was in office over the period 1982–1986, all successive governments have been wrestling with exactly the same difficulties. Public expenditure control, reductions in the minimum wage level, cuts in employers' national insurance contributions, tax changes have all been considered at intervals as ways out of the government's structural dilemma of how to maintain high levels of social provision (to cope with high unemployment and social stress) and yet reduce public spending (to curb the burgeoning public sector borrowing requirement). All have been tried at crisis points, like the fall in oil revenue in 1986 or the 1987 stock market crash, with the exception of a change in the minimum wage level. This was advised by the SER in 1987/1988 but was rejected by the government because of the forthright parliamentary opposition of the ecumenical CDA (Christian Democratic Appeal), the Socialist PvdA (Partij van de Arbeid) and the unions.

The dilemma persists. It is exemplified in the rescue attempts mounted by Dutch governments in respect of Fokker NV (1987) and DAF NV (1992). In the cases of these major companies, the government's purpose was to stave off insolvency – due in no small part to their uncompetitiveness – while preserving as much of the economic potential and social fabric of the companies as was possible. A similar interest in job protection has been displayed in moves inspired by the government at Holland's largest employer, Philips NV at Eindhoven. This company, like so many others in Europe, has been caught up in a long-running struggle to modernize technology and mitigate the ensuing redundancies.

The rank accorded to the Netherlands in the 1992 World Competitiveness Report is better than this appreciation of the Netherlands' problems suggests. At a creditable sixth position, it comes behind Japan, the United States, Denmark, Switzerland and Germany. Nevertheless, and in spite of the country's admitted areas of economic strength, there is undeniably a major problem still to be faced in terms of:

- The costs of the all-embracing social protection system which has been accumulated since 1945. Even though the Dutch PSBR is, as of 1993, under better control than previously, it still involves massive spending which is increasingly becoming unaffordable.
- The relatively high labour costs in Holland. These are made worse by the fact that the minimum wage in the Netherlands is set at a premium level.
- The comparatively low average number of weekly working hours compared with the United States and the Japan. Five weeks' holiday and a 38-hour working week are the norm.

The Netherlands' strong support for the European Charter of Workers' Rights, in general, and the Social Chapter of the Maastricht Treaty, in particular, show just how deeply ingrained politically are concepts of fairness in the distribution of benefit and protection in respect of jobs. It is these very notions which are now being challenged by those in Holland who see their application within industry as leading only to Dutch uncompetitiveness.

Table 9.1 *The power distance scale*[3]

Low power distance	High power distance
Subordinates expect superiors to consult them	Subordinates expect superiors to act autocratically
Ideal superior is a loyal democrat	Ideal superior is a benevolent autocrat

Worse, such critics now see the export of Dutch jobs overseas and eastwards through the outsourcing of components and products which now cost too much to make in the Netherlands.

Human resources management: aspects of the system

Gert Hofstede's seminal research on intercultural comparison[3] deals with two variables which are of great importance for any analysis of human resources management approaches in different countries, namely, power distance and the individualism/collectivism scale. This is an useful model for one to analyse the human resources system in the Netherlands. The first measures the degree to which a business culture in a particular country can be said to be either autocratic (top-down order-giving) or participative (involving those affected by decisions in sharing in making the decision) or intermediate between the polar extremes. The second deals with the relative value placed within the culture in question on the group (family, team, society) and on the individual as a key working player (see Table 9.1).

For Holland, Hofstede's score is 38/80. This denotes a country which does not believe in an extended rank system and dislikes top-down order-giving (i.e. is rather egalitarian in its approach to human relations) and yet has a very strong belief in the freedom of the individual. Although not too much can be read into these figures, they are of interest in reinforcing some of the points that were raised earlier about facets of the Dutch character. The comparable scores for other leading EU countries were:

- Germany 35/67
- Britain 35/89
- France 68/71
- Belgium 65/75

The Dutch level of dichotomy is not as striking as the British. They have a smaller power distance and a higher independence score. In contrast, the French believe in managerial rankings (i.e. they are more autocratic) and have less preference for individual freedom (i.e. they are more bureaucratic).

What is striking is that, however strongly the Dutch seem to believe in personal freedom, they do fear – and fear equally strongly – the consequences of unemployment. Virtually the first element that strikes the outside observer in looking at the Dutch human resource system is the difficulty of sacking workers. The cause is the Law on Labour Conditions (*Arbo Law*). This regulates all matters of health and safety at work in such a way as to ensure a legal framework for the quality of working life. In addition, it gives license to bodies such as SER to discuss all issues related to workers' rights as a matter of principle. Here the critical element under the law is that, in order to make a permanent worker redundant, the company in question needs a permit from the Labour Bureau. This is issued only after justification of the move is given. Should the company need to downsize its workforce, to maintain competitiveness, then the question of workers' rights to their jobs becomes a highly charged union–management one.

Wherever an employee is made redundant and becomes unemployed, he or she is entitled to unemployment pay set at a level related specifically to the final salary. In the 1980s this level was 80 per cent. This effectively removes the incentive to find work that is below one's existing level of qualification.

The right to worker participation in company affairs is safeguarded equally under the 1979 Law on Works Councils (*Wet op de Ondernemingsraden*). This applies to all companies employing more than 100 people. Companies vary in their use of such councils. For some, they offer opportunities for reasoned 'quality circle' consultation about the future. For others, they are a formal forum in which issues of working hours, vacations, pay and personnel policies are agreed. Whatever the use to which they are put, workers have the right to be consulted about all strategic decisions and the right to advise on them. This includes the appointment of senior executives. Naturally, this limits the decisional freedom of shareholders except in some large foreign-owned firms, where the *ondernemingsraden* regulations have been less rigorously applied. However, the Maastricht Treaty reaffirms the strong desire of continental Europe to keep their existing worker participation rules intact and, if anything, to build on them. Additionally, to ensure that they perform well as Council members, worker representatives have the right to be trained. If they need external advisers to help them, the firm must hire them at its cost.

Such *ondernemingsraden* are therefore consulted on all matters of corporate substance – mergers, takeovers, new technology, etc. It should be noted they have certain veto rights in respect of personnel decisions.

The Law on Unfitness for Work (*WAO Law*) makes up the trinity of laws which offer casemate protection to the Dutch worker. This was highly generous in its provision of state benefits, with the government topping up the sickness benefit paid by the firm (70 per cent of income) to 100 per cent for two years. So much so that, in the 1970s and 1980s, some employers pre-ferred to try to put surplus workers on the sick list rather than making them redundant, and the workers themselves welcomed it. This was a policy of choice wherever the unions insisted on extravagant redundancy terms.

If we add together the elements in this picture we cannot avoid the impression of supply-side rigidity, of workforces who have effectively been insulated, over the last 40 years, from economic realities. There is no question but that some of the protection currently given is against the inter-ests of the Netherlands, since it means further erosion of the country's com-petitiveness. How large this problem is looming now is clear from the fact that it was in 1980 that the prestigious government Think Tank, the *Wetenschappelijke Raad voor het Regerings beleid,* published its infamous report on the way in which de-industrialization of the Netherlands was taking place.

Developments in Dutch personnel management

As can be imagined, over time the management of people within Dutch organizations has changed markedly in some ways. Yet in others, particu-larly where subject to protective social legislation and union pressure, there has been little change. Nevertheless, the role of the personnel department has never ceased to have significant importance.

Three periods in the post-war developments of such departments can be distinguished: a foundation (1945–1960), a broadening (1960–1980) and a readjustment (1980+).

In the first of these periods, personnel departments were re-established in major Dutch companies. On the one hand, efficiency and productivity were of prime concern. This gave the department an administrative orientation. Yet simultaneously each firm was required to ingest and apply the battery of new framework laws concerning worker rights, labour conditions and income policies, etc. This placed the department in much more of a gate-keeper role, and this it has never lost.

The years 1960–1980 saw a major broadening of the human resource management function. Under the impulse of breakthrough research in the United States into motivation and job satisfaction, as well in as new forms of organisation structure, human resource specialists improved their skill and knowledge base. Attention was directed particularly to strengthening the identification of employees with their organizations and, from 1979 onwards, to dealing with the creation and handling of works councils. In this they were aided by the trade union movement, whose membership by 1980 numbered some 40 per cent of the Dutch workforce. In the articles of association of most of the unions which are members of the Federation of

Dutch Trade Unions (*Federatie Nederlandsche Vakbeweging*) is commitment to a broad aim that includes support of employers and the improvement of social relations in the workplace. In the same way, internal organizational cultures became areas for research as companies became increasingly concerned with the quality – as opposed to predominantly the quantity – of work.

In their efforts towards improvement companies could count, at this period in Dutch politics, on a continuation of the stable and consistent post-war government in the Netherlands which has resulted, on the one hand, from proportional representation and, on the other, from the pluralist access to the political machine enjoyed by the Dutch Employers Association (*Verbond van Nederlandse Onderneming*) and its trade union counterpart. Thus, leading employers could guarantee in advance a certain predictability in respect of systems for managing labour and for participative decision making. By comparison with Britain, where industrial relations difficulties throughout this period were considerable, the Netherlands was a picture of industrial harmony. Everything – the form of government, government industrial policy, worker protection and participation, the blend of adventurous and sober-minded culture – was of a piece and it looked a good recipe for success.

The third period, which began with the onset of a global recession, has cruelly exposed the obverse of this coin. Personnel departments have, as we have seen in the cases of Fokker and DAF, had to struggle with the fact of receivership in what seemed world-class companies. Philips NV and other leading Dutch firms have gone through a series of restructuring moves to come to terms with the imperative of switching to new technologies such as advanced electronics, informatics and biotechnology. These have created major human resource headaches, especially in management de-layering and re-skilling.

As elsewhere in the European Union personnel issues that have come to the fore are:

- Changes in the nature of work – and the resultant division of labour – as a consequence of shifts in the human–machine balance. As the use of automation has increased (machine), so the need for a large mass of unskilled or semi-skilled labour (human) has fallen. In its place there is a demand for a small volume of multi-skilled, highly qualified workers.
- The extent to which companies have been able to offset the disincentivizing effects of the welfare state by creating a new, result-orientated highly flexible employee.
- Improving corporate competitiveness by negotiating change with unions such as the Christelijk Nationaal Vakverbond and by switching from sectoral to individual company wage bargaining.

This has cast personnel departments in a strategic role. As Vloeberghs put it:[5]

> The emphasis in the period 1960–70 is on the relation between the individual and the organization: the improvement of motivation and job satisfaction, the improvement of relations among employees and of employees and management . . . Personnel managers [in the 1990s] are for the first time confronted with problems of continuity, competitive positions, productivity, quality-assurance, performance criteria, added value and technological imperatives.

No wonder, he adds, that their reaction is one of 'distress and insecurity'.

On the other hand, Misumi's large-scale 1993 research study into comparative attitudes to work[6] indicated that Holland ranked third after Japan and Germany in people's attachment to their work. Perhaps, given the Catholic–Calvinist duality of Dutch religious culture, this should not surprise us. Certainly, it is the case that such commitment is not the product of performance-related pay, merit awards or profit-sharing arrangements for which the take-up in the Netherlands is relatively low.

Even so, personnel managers will increasingly have to deal with phenomena such as the virtual corporation and highly flexible work contracts, as the very nature of organizational life continues to change and as the need to improve Holland's international competitiveness keeps on increasing. The art of managing people will then have to undergo yet another quantum shift. The key question will then be 'Will the socio-industrial approach which the Netherlands has used since 1946 be appropriate to its new tasks?' and the answer will be 'Only the future can tell'.

References

1 Child, J., 'Culture, contingency and capitalism in the cross national study of organisations', in Cummings, L. L. and Staw, B. M. (eds), *Research in Organisational Behaviour*, Vol. 13, pp. 303–356, JAI Press, Greenwich, CT.

2 Dore, R., *British Factory–Japanese Factory: The origins of national diversity in industrial relations*, University of California Press, Berkeley, 1973.

3 Hofstede, G., *Culture's Consequences: International differences in work-related values*, Sage, Beverley Hills, CA, 1980.

4 Nystrom, G. and Starbuck, P., 'Managing beliefs in organisations', *Journal of Applied Behavioural Science* 20(3), 277–287, 1984.

5 Vloeberghs, D., *Human Resource Management*, Acco, Leuven, Belgium, 1989.

6 Misumi, J., 'Attitudes to work in Japan and the West', *Long Range Planning*, **26**, No. 4, 1993.

Index